Therapeutic Parenting

Therapeutic Parenting

⊷⊸⊜⊷⊸

How to Raise an Emotionally Healthy Child

K. H. Kim

HOPEWELL PUBLISHING

Therapeutic Parenting: How to Raise an Emotionally Healthy Child

Inquiries should be addressed to:

Hopewell Publishing
12356 Donovan
Austin, Texas 78753, USA
www.hopewellpublishing.com

First Edition

Cataloging-in-Publication Data

Kim, K. H.
Therapeutic Parenting: How to Raise an Emotionally Healthy Child

      p.   cm.

1. Parenting. 2. Parenting—Psychological aspects. 3. Parent and child. 4. Child
rearing. 5. Family. 6. Child mental health. 7. Adoption. 8. Foster home care.
9. Foster family. 10. Behavioral disorders. 11. Psychotherapy. 12. Play therapy.
I. K. H. Kim. II. Therapeutic Parenting: How to Raise an Emotionally Healthy Child.

ISBN 0-9706820-0-X Pbk

RJ504 K39   649.1 Ki   LC# 00-111959

Although information herein is based on the author's
extensive experience and knowledge, it is not intended
to substitute for the services of qualified professionals.

Printed in the United States of America

*This book is dedicated
to all the beautiful, precious children
of the world and to those of us who love them
unconditionally.*

Acknowledgements

Over the past eight years, I've accumulated all sorts of experience working with children and their parents or caretakers. Some of them have been painful (sometimes, horrible things happened to children, and it was very painful for me to see them suffer emotionally on a day-to-day basis). But most of my experiences with children have been rewarding, and the children have changed my life in more beautiful ways than they'll ever know.

For that, I would like to thank God. And, also, I would like to thank Him for being in my life and for directing my life to the point where I now sit to write this book.

I would like to express my deepest gratitude to my parents, my family and my friends, especially the White Family in No Name, Colorado, for their support and patience throughout my education and ultimately in writing this book.

Additionally, I would like to thank the children and staff at The Women's Center in Fort Worth, Texas for introducing me to the path that I've taken over the years. Also, I would like to express my appreciation to all the children, their parents and the staff at The Women's Shelter in Arlington, Texas for teaching me to be a good therapist and what it means to be truly child-centered.

For my first experience in teaching parenting skills, I would like to thank the parents and staff at the Parenting Center in Fort

Worth. I would also like to acknowledge the numerous child placing agencies, basic care facilities, residential treatment centers, foster parents, adoptive and biological parents for allowing me to go into their agencies or homes so that I could work with their children and their families. I would like to express my sincere appreciation to Marge Georgeson in Austin, Texas for giving me the freedom to focus on my clients over the years.

I would like to recognize the numerous contributions made by the members of the Aspen Writers' Foundation in Colorado for their patience, encouragement and feedback, which are reflected in the following pages. Credit goes to Kira Hultsman for her assistance during the research and for her help on the manuscript for this book.

I would like to thank Mindy Reed of The Authors' Assistant in Austin, Texas for her editing and for her dedication to the publication of this book. I would also like to thank the author Irwin Tang for his valuable guidance during the making of this book.

Lastly, I would like to acknowledge all the parents and caretakers charged with raising our children, for providing love and safety for our kids in need. Thank you for your commitment to helping our children.

Contents

❖❖❖

Acknowledgements 7
Introduction 11
How to Use This Book 16
Disclaimer 17

Part One
Fundamental Parenting Skills

1. Understanding Your Child's Cognitive
   Developmental Stages 21
2. Basic Parenting Skills 25
3. Communication 31
4. How to be a Positive Role Model 42
5. Using Natural and Logical Consequences 49
6. Teaching Children Age-Appropriate Social Skills 65
7. Increasing Your Child's Self-Esteem 70
8. Additional Parenting Techniques 76

Part Two
Therapeutic Parenting Skills

A Word of Warning 83
9. Attention-Deficit/Hyperactivity Disorder (ADHD)
   and Oppositional Behaviors 85

10. Children with Serious Conduct Problems 90
11. Sexually Abused Children 103
12. Physically Abused Children 121
13. Children with Depression 127
14. Children of Divorce 131
15. When There is a Death in the Family 137
16. Bed-wetting 142
17. Children Who Lack Age-Appropriate Social Skills ... 147
18. Sibling Conflict 152
19. The Problem with Tattling 156
20. Anxiety 158
21. Separation Anxiety 171
22. School Problems 177
23. Children with Low Self-Esteem 182
24. Special Issues Related to Therapeutic Parenting 189
25. Conclusion 204

Appendix 205
Bibliography 208
Index 210

Introduction

⊷⟫⊜⟪⊶

Parents don't *intend* to be "bad parents." I've worked with many parents, from foster parents to biological parents, who have had their children returned to them by a child protective agency. Every one of these parents loved their children and wanted what was best for them.

It's true that some parents don't go through life asking, "What do I do about my child's problem with stealing?" Or, "What do I do about my child's depression?" "What if my child is sexually abused, or what if he sexually abuses another child?" Most parenting books do not address these issues. Nonetheless, these questions are real, and they are asked more often than our society feels comfortable admitting. Admitting that there are sexually abused children in our communities or that children take their lives at age thirteen is hard to do.

A child's economic, educational or social standing does not make him or her immune to these problems. One particular issue may affect one group of children more than another group, but the sad truth is that these problems affect many children each and every day.

Therapeutic Parenting is a practical "How To" guide for addressing these real problems. The purpose of this book is to aid parents, foster parents and other adults in their commitment to help children. In this book you will learn how to detect if your child has serious emotional or behavioral needs. This book offers various creative and therapeutic parenting skills that can help children work through their problems. It's also about how to talk to your child so that you may, with grace and skill, improve your child's life.

What is Therapeutic Parenting?

Therapeutic parenting is a method of parenting that requires parents to change their own behavior, and not just that of their children. Therapeutic parenting involves parents being creative in their parenting strategies in order to address their children's constantly changing emotional and behavioral needs.

Research indicates that a combination of medication and therapeutic parenting skills is one of the most effective approaches for helping children with behavioral problems, such as Attention-Deficit/Hyperactivity Disorder (ADHD). It has been my experience that the progress children make in therapy depends largely on the therapist's communication with the parents, and in many instances, progress can be made only if parents themselves participate in the sessions.

Several years ago, I was asked to provide a six-week parent training program to a biological mom. Her 6-year-old daughter had been extremely hyperactive, physically aggressive and defiant. The mother reacted to these behaviors by physically abusing her, resulting in a child protective agency removing her daughter from the home.

The mother was highly motivated to be reunited with her child. She completed all the requirements set by the courts, and during the reunification process she even developed a good working relationship with her child's foster parents. After the reunification, I stepped in solely to provide the mother with parenting skills training. We had a rough beginning, and the mother was unsure if she could "handle" her daughter during the initial session. However, through parenting skills training and direct hands-on coaching in their home environment, she was able to complete the program successfully. About a couple of weeks later, the child's ex-foster dad told me that he was so impressed with this mom's new parenting skills, that he would trust her to provide respite care for the other eight foster children in his home.

My initial intent was to write this book based mostly on scholarly journal articles and other "technical" books written for professionals. However, as I started working on the book, I realized that most of what I wanted to say in this book came not from scholarly journals or technical books, but from my own personal and professional experience with children.

When I was in graduate school at The University of Texas at Arlington, I was required to complete two internships in order to graduate with a Master's degree in Social Work. Since the age of thirteen, I had wanted to be a therapist. So I chose to do both of my internships at a non-profit counseling center.

In 1991, I began my first internship at the Community Service Clinic in Arlington. Here, I had my first experience as a therapist and my first experience in working with children. I did my second internship at the Parenting Center in Fort Worth. I chose the Parenting Center not because I wanted to work with children or parents, but because it was the only agency available for me to develop and practice my counseling skills.

My plan was to work with articulate, educated and intelligent adults, with whom I could talk about the inner psyche and philosophize about the struggles of life. However, fate had another plan for me.

When I first began working at the Parenting Center, I felt lost and insecure about my abilities as a therapist, even with the experience of my first internship under my belt. But the staff at the Parenting Center took me under their wing and encouraged me to grow both professionally and personally. It was at this agency that I had my first experience teaching parenting skills.

I didn't know if what I was teaching the parents was really effective. But I continued to teach these skills as part of my assignment. Then, one day, some of the parents came up to me, excited about what I'd been teaching them. "It works! You wouldn't believe the changes in my son," they said. Well, the excitement got to me. Their enthusiasm rubbed off on me, and I was gung-ho about parenting classes from that day forth.

In December 1992, my internship ended, and I left the Parenting Center and graduated with my degree. After the graduation, I got a job at a nursing home, not providing therapy, as I wanted to, but doing administrative work because I needed to pay off my student loans.

Some time went by before I made up my mind to put aside my need for financial security to do what I loved the most. I started looking in the newspaper for the words, "Therapist Needed." I didn't care where I had to work, and I didn't care how much it paid.

I saw an ad for a child therapist position at the Rape Crisis in Fort Worth. This is where my life changed forever, for good. The children at the Rape Crisis taught me about grace, about strength and forgiveness, and about truly connecting with people. They were my role model for how I wanted to be the rest of my life.

I found myself, and I found my freedom through the eyes of these children, through their loving and innocent wisdom. After some time, I transferred my remaining clients to my co-workers and left for Europe to celebrate my freedom in having found my identity.

Several months later, I came back and went back to work. Again, I chose a position for financial reasons. It wasn't exactly what I was looking for. But, here, I had my first experience with children who had severe emotional and behavioral problems. I traveled all over Texas to be an advocate for these children for over a year. I visited numerous foster homes, child placing agencies, basic care facilities and residential treatment centers to make sure the children at these places were taken care of.

I left this agency because of a move to another city. About a year after the move, I started working at a private practice, and then a few months later, I began to live my dream. I opened my own private practice, not working with adults as I had hoped in my childhood, but with children. But, by this time, I preferred to work with children. They made better clients, and they were more fun to work with. Even to this day, I tell my child clients, "I have the best job in the whole wide world. I get to play with kids and talk to kids, and get paid for it!"

For the past three and half years, I've seen hundreds of biological, foster and adopted children in my practice. I have had the luxury of seeing some of them in my office. However, I saw most of my clients in their home or school environment. I traveled up to two hours one-way, twice or even three times a week, to see my clients and their families.

I've worked with countless numbers of biological parents, foster and adoptive parents, caseworkers and case managers, teachers, counselors and principals, as well as a number of CASA workers and attorneys. I've consulted with numerous parents and taught them creative parenting skills. For the past couple of years, I've expanded to teaching larger groups of parents by providing parenting skills classes.

I wrote this book with the hope that I might expand even further and reach parents worldwide. This book is based on my experiences with children and their families over the past eight years. I hope what I have to share with you will help you become more capable, loving parents.

How to Use This Book

⊷⟞⊜⊙⟞⟝⊷

I recommend reading the chapters on cognitive developmental stages and fundamental parenting skills first and then moving on to specific problem areas. Part One contains primarily hypothetical situations and is intended for any parent or caretaker. This section of the book serves as a foundation for the remainder of the book, because it contains information that you will need whether your child is occasionally oppositional or involved in illegal activities.

In Part Two, I address different problematic behaviors in children as well as some of the more prevalent issues that children face today. These chapters are based on my professional experience with clients, although their names and any identifying information have been changed in order to preserve confidentiality. In this part of the book, you'll learn how to parent children effectively and "therapeutically" and how you can communicate with them at different developmental levels.

Disclaimer

⊷══◉ ◉══⊷

This book is intended as a "How To" guide for parenting children. Its purpose is not to make the reader into a therapist. There is not a set way to parent children. To claim such would be unrealistic and, frankly, untrue. However, the messages in this book are based on my professional experience over the past eight years, and the techniques outlined in this book have been highly successful in helping parents raise emotionally healthy children.

Some of the suggestions given may prove to be successful in working with a particular child. If not, you may want to try out other methods outlined in this book. All children are different, and it may take a different approach with one child versus another child.

Parents may learn the same parenting techniques. However, due to a wide range of personalities, as well as different dynamics involved in each family, a particular approach may be highly useful and effective in one family but not in another. Again, you may want to refer to various skills outlined in the book to discover what works best for your family.

I highly recommend that this book be used in conjunction with therapy provided by an experienced professional. The techniques in this book do not address the specific nature of your child's problems or the dynamics present in your family. Only an experienced therapist can address these issues.

I wrote this book with every intention of helping parents and caregivers communicate with and parent their children more effectively. Whatever harm or misunderstanding that may come after reading this book is entirely unintentional. My approach throughout the book has been to proceed with caution in order to safeguard your child, as well as your family. *Please note that in agreeing to read this book, you understand and accept that I (or anyone representing or associated with this book) am not responsible for any damages—emotional, financial or otherwise—incurred after the reading of this book.*

Part One
Fundamental Parenting Skills

Chapter 1

Understanding Your Child's Cognitive Developmental Stages

To understand how therapeutic parenting skills work, parents need to understand the different developmental stages of children. From the time they are born, children develop physically, mentally, emotionally, socially and morally; and all these areas promote or limit one another.

For example, if infants are severely neglected, they often fail to develop physically and mentally on a normal level. This, in turn, affects the other three areas of development, such as their ability to relate to other children.

When I teach parenting skills, parents often ask me: "What's normal for my child at this age?" A brief understanding of children's cognitive development may help answer this question since it serves to further or limit children's development in many of the other areas.

According to Jean Piaget, one of the founding fathers of developmental psychology, children go through four stages of cognitive development. These include the Sensorimotor (birth to 2-year-old), Preoperational (2-year-old to 7-year-old), Concrete Operations (7-year-old to 11-year-old), and Formal Operations (11-year-old and beyond).

Sensorimotor Stage

During the Sensorimotor stage, infants experience their world through their five senses. They take in their surrounding and incorporate their new experiences through what they can see, hear, smell, taste and touch. At the end of this stage, they are capable of "complex sensorimotor coordination." They learn to sit, crawl and walk. These infants also learn what's called "object permanence." They realize that objects continue to exist even when they are out of sight.

Preoperational Stage

By the time children enter the Preoperational stage, they're able to use images and language to experience and to interact with the world. They respond to their environment according to the way things appear to be to them and not necessarily how things really are. They're able to use imagination in their play and in their interaction with others. This is the stage in which children can start responding to activities, such as play therapy which relies on their ability to use their imagination to help them process their feelings and acquire new coping skills.

At this age, they believe that everyone sees the world as they see the world. But, towards the end of this stage, they begin to realize that people may not always see the world as they do.

Concrete Operations Stage

During the Concrete Operations stage, children begin to think logically, and they can calculate things and understand things based on their ability to do so. They do not automatically accept things based on appearances. And they begin to think about *motivations* behind one's behavior at this stage.

Formal Operations Stage

According to Piaget, during the Formal Operations stage adolescents can engage in systematic and abstract thoughts. Their thinking is not limited to concrete observable things or events. At this stage, children begin to think about what's also possible. Like scientists, they're capable of using systematic deductive reasoning to come up with many possible solutions to a problem or many possible interpretations of an event.

As noted previously, a child's cognitive level is intertwined with and affects other areas of development. In other words, a child's social or emotional response depends largely on his cognitive development.

For instance, we can't expect a 5-year-old child to share his toys because that's the altruistic thing to do. However, we can expect him to share his toys in order to avoid logical consequences (see Chapter 5 on "Using Natural and Logical Consequences"). He knows that if he fights over the toys, he won't be able to play with them, until he gets another chance to share his toys five minutes later. He decides to share his toys with others not because it's a good thing to do (which points to his limited moral development) but because he doesn't want to lose the privilege of playing with his toys.

He decides to share his toys, even though he's angry about having to share them with others. Anger would be an appropriate response in this situation for a 5-year-old. But he still chooses to avoid the less desirable emotional consequence of not being able to play with his toys altogether.

Similarly, we can't expect a 3-year-old child or even a 5-year-old child, to keep her room spotless. However, we can expect a 13-year-old to clean his room and to do his own laundry. The 5-year-old may be limited by her development. Conversely, the 13-year-old may be limited by his motivation. Just because he can clean his room or do his laundry doesn't guarantee that he will. Here's where parenting skills can come in handy. You can actually increase his motivation to do his chores.

Because of the limited cognitive development of the 5-year-old, you may need to show her how she should clean her room. You may pick up some of the toys and put them in the toy box, as you explain to her, "This is where you put your toys, in the toy box!" But with the 13-year-old, it would be sufficient, at least you hope, to *tell* him how he should clean his room.

Parents and caretakers have the power to affect their children's personalities, temperaments and, most importantly, their behaviors. This can be accomplished by changing how they relate to their children.

Parents can nurture children with love, kindness, encouragement and acceptance. But they can also guide and teach them so that they can learn the difference between right and wrong, what is appropriate and what is inappropriate. They can also teach children to respond differently to their emotions. For example, children can learn to express their anger with words, rather than with physical aggression.

Chapter 2

Basic Parenting Skills

Creating Change

You may want your child to change, and probably for good reasons. It's reasonable for you to want him to respect you and to comply with what you are asking him to do. There's nothing wrong with wanting children to mature and become responsible.

If you want your child to change, if you want to improve your relationship, you have to change the way you relate to him. You cannot expect him to change if you continue to do the same things. If the relationship is to improve, both parties have to change the way they behave and the way they relate to each other.

This may seem like an impossible task because as a society we are used to relating to young people in certain ways. It may feel uncomfortable, or even unnatural, to relate to them differently. Many parents complain that they feel like they're "faking it" when they first try to use new parenting skills. Sometimes, they say, "But that's just not the way I talk naturally." My usual response is, "I understand it may feel unnatural. But if the way you relate to each other isn't working for *either* of you, why not try something new?"

It is normal to feel uncomfortable with change. Most adults are following their own parents' style of parenting. What feels natural to them is what has been ingrained in them since childhood. Therefore, parents may have to "fake it" until the new skills become natural to them. Change comes from learning and using these new parenting skills. Once parents realize how effective these skills can be in getting children to respond positively, they will want to continue using them. Through faith, practice and patience, your relationship can improve, the way you want it to be.

The Importance of Bonding

Whether you are trying to parent your biological, adoptive or foster children, it's very important to establish a bond with them. There are several ways to do this. You can give them rewards, praises or privileges, or you can participate in recreational activities on a one-to-one basis or as a family unit. In many families, the members bond with each other during dinnertime or by cooking together.

But there are other subtle ways to bond with children. Many parents find it difficult to talk to their kids unless it's about doing their household chores or their homework. The kids, in turn, may interpret this as "nagging." And this further widens the emotional gap between parents and their children.

One way to counter this is by talking to children and teenagers about other things of interest to them such as sports, television shows, teen fashion, music, or, if they are willing, about their friends. Having conversations with them is not done with the intention of becoming their friends, but parents don't have to perceive their roles strictly as disciplinarians.

It's okay to have fun with your children, and it's okay to just chitchat with them. My teenage clients enjoy hearing about my interests or about my perspective on things. And I don't have to always give advice in order to be a good therapist for them. Sometimes, I even share my worries or concerns, and I remember to ask them to help me as well.

I do a lot of research on what my clients find interesting. For my younger clients, I watch Saturday morning and after-school cartoons, so I can talk to them about these programs. For example,

I went through several decks of Pokemon cards, so I could memorize the names of all the different characters. With one of my more difficult clients, I was finally able to break through to him by having a contest on who could name more of the characters.

To relate to my teenage clients, I listen to the Backstreet Boys and 'NSYNC and watch teen TV shows. A couple of years ago, I actually brought myself to watch "Beavis and Butthead." I didn't like the show, but at least I knew what my clients were talking about.

Being Child-Centered

Parenting children effectively requires being "child-centered." That means understanding how children think and what motivates them to behave in a certain way.

Most parents find it easy to learn new parenting skills, just as they learned multiplication tables in grade school. However, if they still have a problem understanding their children, they might find themselves even more frustrated, as they wonder why the new skills aren't working.

Take comfort in knowing that children often get worse before they get better. As with anyone, any type of change can be difficult, even if it's in their best interests. They may "get worse" in order to resist the change, because it feels uncomfortable to relate to their parents in a new way. But, with persistence, on both the parents' and their children's part, the new way of relating to each other can become "natural." Understanding this process can help parents persevere in their efforts to be skilled parents.

Parents need to understand children and the motivations behind their misbehaviors. This understanding will allow parents to use the skills they have learned, within the appropriate context, to be more effective in altering their children's behaviors.

Example

Five-year-old Lisa refuses to eat her broccoli. This is surprising because Lisa usually likes broccoli. Her dad, Jim thinks, "Oh, good! Here's my chance to use the reward system I learned in the parenting class." So, he calmly tells his daughter, "Lisa, you can have ice-cream after you eat your broccoli."

To Jim's surprise, Lisa does not respond positively. In fact, she starts screaming, "Please, Dad, don't make me eat the broccoli."

In this situation Jim should stay cool and try to understand Lisa's seemingly unreasonable behavior. By talking to Lisa, he will learn that she almost choked on her broccoli yesterday at the babysitter's. So before thinking "tantrum control," Jim could say, "Lisa, I see you don't want any broccoli today. You usually love broccoli. What happened?" This gives Lisa an opportunity to tell him what happened, and it allows Jim to validate her feelings (to validate one's feelings means to acknowledge one's feelings as being legitimate).

Understanding children is crucial in interpreting their behavior. Learning what motivates them will assist parents in their commitment to becoming more capable and caring parents.

Being child-centered does not mean that a parent has to give in to whatever a child wants. Instead, it means stepping into the child's world to understand and guide her behavior. It means taking into account the child's age and her developmental level to understand the motivation behind her inappropriate behavior.

Being child-centered helps parents remember what it felt like to be a child. Looking at a situation through a child's eyes takes into account the child's physical, cognitive, emotional, social and moral developmental levels. This allows parents to form realistic expectations about their child's behaviors.

Example

Joey, a 6-year-old, is crying because he misplaced one of his three Pikachu cards from his Pokemon collection. His mother, Sally wonders, "What's the big deal? He has two other cards that are exactly the same."

She could say, "Oh Sweetie, it's okay. Look, you have two other cards that are exactly the same." But Joey may continue to cry and demand the missing card, setting up a situation for an ongoing argument.

In contrast, Sally could say. "Oh Joey, I know that was your favorite card. I'm sorry you lost it."

In this response, Sally is stepping into Joey's world, a world in which Pokemon cards are very important. She is focusing on his feelings based on what's important to him, rather than what *she* thinks is important. When she validates his feelings, Sally is being child-centered. She is letting him know that his feelings are okay and this, in turn, will help him feel better and move on to another subject.

Summary: Being child-centered means

- Understanding what motivates your child.
- Stepping into a child's world to understand his/her feelings and thoughts.
- Being able to understand the meaning of your child's inappropriate behaviors.
- Not giving in to whatever your child wants.
- Remembering to take into account a child's developmental level in having realistic expectations and in giving out logical consequences or rewards.

The Importance of being Consistent

In parenting children, it is very important to be as consistent as possible. You may change your approach as they get older regarding setting their limits, rewards or consequences (see Chapter 5 on "Using Natural and Logical Consequences"). Although there'll be changes as they mature, you should still be consistent in following through. Otherwise, it'll be difficult for them to trust you and for them to rely on you to guide them though their difficulties.

If you are not consistent, the problematic behaviors can actually get worse. Therefore, if you give in and buy the lollipop for your child because he's been crying for the last 15 minutes, you are actually teaching him to persevere against resistance. He may learn that if he cries loud enough or long enough, that maybe you will give in this time. He doesn't know when he can count on you to give in, so he "ups" the undesirable behavior in the hope that he might be rewarded.

You have to take the time to be reliable and follow through with the consequences each time children engage in inappropriate behaviors. If you are inconsistent, they may think that you will "let it go just this time" and take their chances.

It's also important to be consistent between all caretakers. The mom and dad should agree on the rules, consequences and rewards. Ideally, they should share responsibility in all of these areas. If not, there should be some understanding between the parents, as well as the children, that mom rules over certain areas and dad rules over the other areas.

These areas should be small in number. This is important in order to avoid "splitting." Splitting happens when our children try to work one parent or a caretaker against another. A classic example of this is when a teenager argues, "But Dad, Mom said I could do it!" when he knows very well that Mom didn't say anything remotely close to this.

If you want a happy child, work on your marriage first. When children see that their parents love and respect each other and that their parents work as a team, they feel more happy and secure.

Another example of splitting occurs when a child's favorite aunt either forgets the rules or purposely goes against the rules set by the parents. You don't have to raise your voice or be disrespectful towards the aunt, especially in front of the children. Instead, you can remind her of the rules and inform her that the rules stand, as is, when they concern your children. If she doesn't respect your wishes, then you know better than to leave your children alone with her in the future.

Chapter 3

Communication

Communicating Effectively
with Children

In communicating with children, it's important to remember to use developmentally appropriate words. If a child does not understand what is being said, the point will be lost even if the message is right. Additionally, you may want to sit on the floor when talking to very young children. You'll be able to maintain eye contact, which is critical to determining whether or not your child heard or understood your message.

Example

Jane is in the kitchen cooking dinner, when she sees her 5-year-old son throwing his sister's toy against the living room wall. She yells across the room, "Billy, I was very disappointed with how you handled that situation. I think it was very inappropriate." In this instance, Billy will know that Jane is angry from her tone of voice, but he won't understand why she is angry.

Instead, Jane could come into the living room and get down on his level. She could look him in the eyes and say, "Billy, I don't like it when you break your sister's toys. I know you're mad at her. Tell her how you feel with words." In this example, Jane is brief and direct, so Billy will understand why she is disappointed. More importantly, he will know how to cope with his anger appropriately in the future.

In parenting classes, I tell parents that if they go beyond three or four sentences while redirecting their child (especially with a teenager), it automatically becomes a lecture. Whatever is said beyond this limit doesn't register in the child's brain.

I interviewed several teenagers for this book. I told them that their opinions would be representing other teenagers nationwide. I knew they were hesitant and a little nervous about the interview. So I used a little bit of humor and addressed their concerns by exaggerating their worries. Everybody laughed and my exaggeration helped to put the teenagers at ease.

I asked them for their opinions on what parents should learn about parenting today's teens. One of them commented, "Everything!" Another one said, "I don't know." I told them that I wasn't looking for a standard teenager response and that I really wanted to know what they had to say on the subject. After much debate, we came up with a tentative title for the project, "How to Interpret Your Teenager."

Several of them explained that "I don't know," "I don't remember," and "I forget" all mean, "Leave me alone." However, another teenager commented, "It all depends on how we say these things. "I don't know," could mean "Leave me alone," but it could also mean, "Keep asking."

The boys never agreed on the exact meaning of "I don't know." However, it is evident from their responses that parents have to develop a special kind of relationship or understanding with their teenagers. It is the only way to know when they say one thing but may mean another.

In my experience as a therapist, it seems that teenagers want to talk, although they may try to indicate otherwise. I believe they just want some encouragement to open up and assurance that I really want to listen to what they have to say. And once they open up, they keep talking. I've had to escort some teenage clients out because they wouldn't stop talking at the end of our session.

When talking to teenagers, do not assume anything. The key is to really listen to them without interrupting or being judgmental. Also it's important to be genuine in your responses without being too emotional.

Although it may be very difficult to remain calm at times and be genuine about their feelings, parents can still communicate their expectations with phrases such as "I would prefer" or "I would like," rather than "I expect." The first two phrases are assertive, and they still keep the lines of communication open.

Example

Sixteen-year-old Kristen comes home at midnight, two hours past her curfew. Without yelling or pointing her finger, her mother Ginger says, "I'm glad you're safe, but I was very worried about you. Why don't we talk about this tomorrow since it's late? Maybe we can work something out that will work for both of us in the future."

This may sound like an unrealistic or impossible response, especially when you have been gripped with fear of the unknown and angry about being disobeyed. However, by practicing to stay calm and learning to use this approach, you can become more objective. Your emotions are kept in check, allowing you to respond to your teenager's behaviors and not react to them.

In this interaction, Ginger was not letting Kristen get away with breaking the curfew. Remember, they are going to continue the conversation the following day. Ginger would have been unproductive if she insisted on talking about the matter so late in the evening, especially when her emotions had been stretched beyond the rational point.

By waiting until the next morning, Ginger can prevent regretting what she might have said to Kristen in anger, which would have only escalated the situation. Ginger, after reflection, can respect that Kristen made a choice, but that choice may now result in consequences. Using this approach, Ginger can teach

Kristen that choices lead to consequences (see Chapter 5 on "Using Natural and Logical Consequences"). Based on how well Ginger knows her daughter and her daughter's motivations, she may allow Kristen to recommend her own consequences.

Sometimes, a parent may feel insecure or uncomfortable relating to their teenagers in a new way. It may be difficult, but it's extremely important not to show fear. A timid voice while carrying out logical consequence (see Chapter 5 on "Using Natural and Logical Consequences") is not as effective as a confident and calm voice.

As with any skill, practice is the key to success. It may help to practice what you want to say to them in front of a mirror, or you can practice with your spouse or other adults and ask for their feedback. Their comments may not be as helpful, compared to a teenager's feedback, but it helps to have another person's input when you attempt to improve your communication skills.

Over the years, I've adopted some creative methods of communicating with children and teens. Sometimes, I've invented new approaches on the spot, used shocking statements or given them unexpected responses to get my message across. There are many different ways to approach this based on the circumstances and based on the personality of the child.

This part of the chapter will focus on three major areas of communication. You will learn how to praise children, how to confront them and how to say "no" where they can understand that "no" means "no!"

Children should be praised when they've accomplished a task, when they've given their best at something or when they have exhibited or attempted to show good character.

When I see a child trying her best or trying something new, even though she feels scared or insecure, I go out of my way to praise her. When a child is helpful, considerate or compassionate towards other, I praise for that too.

The following is a list of examples I may use to praise a child:

- "Good job!"

- "You are amazing!"
- "Okay, impress me again!"
- "Now, how'd you get to be so smart!?!"
- "Now, what did I tell you about being so good!?!"
- "I am just sooo proud of you!"
- "Do you know how great you are?"
- "You are just sooo good, I almost can't stand it!"
- "You have to be the greatest kid in the whole world!"
- "Okay, now you're going to make me cry. I'm just sooo proud of you!"
- "Hey, I wanna be just like you when I grow up!"

Most of the above examples are appropriate for younger children. However, by altering some of the words, you can communicate the same message to teenagers.

Sometimes, children have a hard time accepting "no" from their parents. Changing their parents' minds becomes more of a priority than their desire to carry out the original act. Some of them even resort to manipulation to get their way. They may become very inventive in their excuses for not doing their homework, their chores or for not following instructions.

It is easy for parents to fall for their excuses or naively give into their manipulations. Children can be charming. So, it is important to become keen in being able to identify their attempts to excuse their behaviors or their attempts to have their way.

When a child has difficulty accepting a refusal, an appropriate response may be "Na-ah!" And if she persists, "Let me say it another way. *Nooooo!*" These still get the message across, but they also use a sense of humor to maintain good rapport.

If a child tries to manipulate or insists on something, try using the following:

- "Good try. But the answer is still *no!*"
- "It almost worked, but not quite. Better luck next time!"
- "Okay. Try it again."

- "Okay. Next topic?"

Sometimes children can come up with some of the most remarkable excuses for not doing their chores or for not meeting some other expectations. In this case, you may want to respond with the following examples:

- "Don't even go there!"

- "Oh, please! You can come up with a better excuse than that."

- "Oh, stop right there while you're still cold!"

Remember, even young children respond to humor and irony. For example, if a child drops something on the floor and doesn't pick it up, you might say, "Oh, no, no, *no*. Please don't get up. Let me get that for you...Not!" If he avoids doing his homework, "Oh, let me do your homework for you today!" Or if he "forgets" to take the trash out or neglects to clean his room, try asking, "Did the trash man go on strike today, or did the maid not show up again today?"

Before using these approaches, make sure the child will understand your intent. Otherwise, they may be confused or offended by what is said. These responses help to remind them they have to work harder than they think to avoid their responsibilities. Eventually, most children will give in and resume their responsibilities.

Summary:

- Use developmentally appropriate words.

- Get down on their level to maintain eye contact.

- Be brief as possible, especially during a request or in carrying out logical consequences.

- Develop and maintain a good rapport.

- Make an effort to be gentle or playful.

- Take into account non-verbal communication to interpret what children are actually saying.

- Match your verbal communication with your non-verbal communication.
- Remain calm and objective, while still being genuine about your feelings and expectations.
- Do not assume things, and try to refrain from being judgmental.
- Be courageous and matter-of-fact when confronting children.
- Postpone confrontation when your emotions are out of control.

Praising Children Appropriately

The most important thing I have to say about using praises is to use them generously. But be honest in praising children. Don't praise them if you don't mean it, or if they don't deserve it.

If your words don't match the tone of your voice, facial expression or body gestures as you praise them, children are not going to believe what you say. When you are proud of a child's accomplishments, you can tell her you are proud of her as you smile and pat her on the back.

Sometimes, parents tell me that they're running out of things to praise their child about, especially if he's acting out more so than usual. In this case praise him about *anything and everything*. If he's totally focused on playing the video game, praise him for his ability to focus. If he's watching the TV quietly, praise him for his consideration towards others. Obviously he's not doing anything extraordinary, but he's not tearing the TV set apart to see how it works either. In this case, you should actively look for things to praise him about. You would be surprised just how many things you can be proud of if you intentionally take the time to look for positive behaviors.

I know that it seems like a stretch, but some stretching may be necessary when trying to encourage children to engage in positive behaviors. As they get used to the praises and look forward to the praises, they'll hopefully go out of their way to do other positive things. For instance, a child may take out the trash without being asked first. So, go out of your way with the praises. The next day he might surprise you by vacuuming the whole house!

Praises are a form of "social rewards." By praising children, you are basically teaching them to do what's socially appropriate, even if they're not rewarded with material things. They eventually learn that they can receive approval and recognition from society for doing the right thing.

Case Study

A few months ago, I had the privilege of working with a couple who are wonderful adoptive parents. They had recently adopted a 6-year-old girl named Jasmine who turned out to be a little more challenging than they originally thought. Jasmine had major control issues.

During the first family session, I noticed that her mother, Yolanda, praised Jasmine almost constantly. I thought, "Oh my gosh, this can't be real!" I thought that Yolanda was the best adoptive parent I'd ever seen.

Between the first and the second session, I received a call from her. I could tell she was trying hard to be positive. However, I sensed her frustration in working with Jasmine. I told her that I was impressed with how she acknowledged Jasmine during the first session. Yolanda told me that she was trying her best in order to increase Jasmine's self-esteem. However, she told me that no matter how much she tried to help Jasmine, that she still behaved inappropriately most of the time at home.

As we continued our conversation, a question flashed across my mind. What motivated Jasmine to behave negatively even though her adoptive mother was showering her with praises? I told Yolanda to continue praising her, but I also suggested that she interact with Jasmine sometimes without constantly praising her.

I thought that Jasmine might have been anxious about having to perform for her adoptive parents. She might have misunderstood the praises as Yolanda's way of telling her that her worth was "performance-based," although this clearly wasn't Yolanda's intention.

I recommended that she praise Jasmine indirectly at times. For example, she could praise Jasmine by saying, "I have so much fun when I'm with you! I love talking to you!"

Two weeks later, Yolanda informed me that Jasmine's behavior had improved tremendously since our telephone conversation. She believed that changing her strategy and the way she praised Jasmine accounted for the dramatic improvement in Jasmine's behavior.

Summary:

- Praise children generously.
- Your tone of voice, facial expression and body gestures should match what you say when you are praising children.
- Actively look for things for which you can praise your children.
- Praises are a form of a "social reward" and can replace material rewards as your children get older.

Teaching Children to Express Their Feelings

When you teach a child to express his feelings and when you acknowledge his feelings, you can help reduce his misbehavior by as much as seventy-five percent. In the previous example using the Pokemon cards, just validating the child's feelings prevented an argument.

Example

Seven-year-old Suzy has fallen off her bicycle. Her father Ken might say, "Now, Suzy, I told you to watch where you're going! That's what you get for not paying attention. Now stop your crying!"

Suzy might cry louder and argue, "But I was watching where I was going!"

In contrast, Ken could say, "Oh, Suzy, that must have hurt. Let me give you a hug. Now, where are you hurt?"

Suzy may sniffle a bit and point to the area on her knee. "Right here."

"Ouch! That does look like it hurts." Then Ken could continue, "I cry sometimes when I'm hurting or when I'm sad. Sometimes, crying makes me feel better, and sometimes telling someone how I feel makes me feel better. Next time, when you get hurt or when you feel sad, you can come tell Mommy or me. Say, 'Daddy, I feel sad because I hurt myself.' Okay?"

Example

Six-year-old Toby hits his brother for snatching his toy away. His mother, Helen could say, "Toby, I can tell you're very angry, but tell your brother how you feel with words." If Toby has difficulty with this concept, Helen can model for him how he should talk to his brother. "You can say, 'Dillon, I feel really mad when you take my things away without asking me. Next time, I want you to ask me first.'" And then, Helen should praise Toby or hug him when he does express his feelings appropriately.

It's important that children are allowed to express their feelings fully. In order to do this, parents and adults must first restrain themselves from interrupting them and telling them how they should feel.

There is no such thing as right or wrong feelings. Feelings are just feelings. However, feelings may be based on misunderstandings or some other faulty beliefs. Therefore, the focus should be on correcting the misunderstanding of faulty beliefs, and not the feelings.

For instance, if you go out to the driveway and see that your car is missing, it is understandable if you feel angry or violated, especially if you think it was stolen. It's unrealistic for anyone to expect you to change your feelings about the situation. However, if you find out that your spouse took the car to go get some milk, your feelings will probably change. You may feel slightly irritated with your spouse, rather than angry or violated.

Summary:

In teaching children to express their feelings appropriately,

- Acknowledge and validate their feelings, even if you disagree with them.

- Do not minimize or negate their feelings, and avoid telling them how they should feel, even if you are trying to help them feel better.

- Show them how they can express their feelings with words, instead of acting out their feelings through negative behaviors.

- Encourage them to express their feelings appropriately by praising them and acknowledging them when they do express their feelings directly.

Chapter 4

How to be a Positive Role Model

Encouraging and Motivating
Your Children

Children cannot be supervised 24 hours a day, at least in the home environment. Therefore, it's necessary that they learn to monitor and manage their behavior on their own, without constant supervision.

It is unrealistic to expect a 5-year-old or even an 11-year-old to do what's appropriate consistently even under someone's guidance. However, there are some skills you can help her develop so that she will have a better chance of being able to maintain her own behavior without someone watching and directing her every step.

You can encourage and motivate your child to do the right thing even when she's not being watched. I have had great success by "over-praising" children when they engage in appropriate behaviors. When I see them cooperating with each other, I like to go overboard and pat them on the back as I praise them repeatedly.

I let them know, "Oh, I just *love* it when you help your sister! You are such a good helper!" With teenagers, I use a slightly different approach. I might say, "You know, I really appreciate you helping me." For emphasis, I might briefly pat them on the back as I let them know how much I appreciate them.

My favorite way to motivate young people is by praising them generously and by showing them attention and appreciation when I catch them helping others (you'll be surprised how many good things you can catch your child doing if you just look for them). When they share their toys, you can praise them; when they do their homework without being asked, praise them again; if you see a child studying hard, you can say, "You're such a hard worker," as you pat them on the back.

Case Study

I had a client who was 18 years old and about to graduate from high school. Gabe had been in special education for some of his classes throughout high school, and towards the end of his senior year, he became highly anxious because he wasn't sure if he would "make it out in the real world."

I validated and normalized his feelings, and then explained to him that I had gone through a similar crisis during my senior year in high school. I also talked about his strengths and his past achievements to let him know that *I* had faith he would "make it out in the real world."

He agreed with me by the end of the session, but then he showed the same insecurities during our next session. This time, he asked me to "keep on" telling him about the things I talked about during our last session. He wanted me to remind him of his strengths and to encourage him to go out there to achieve his dreams. And I did.

About a couple of months later, the time came for his graduation. He invited me to the graduation ceremony. I had to refuse, but I told him that I would be with him in spirit. Several weeks later, I received a graduation picture of my client from his ex-foster parents, and I knew he would "make it" out there.

The best way to help children to be responsible and to make good choices is by being an inspiring role model (refer to "About Choices and Responsibility" under Chapter 5). Role modeling is one of the most important parenting skills you will ever learn, because it forces you to practice what you preach. If you find yourself in a situation where you are not practicing what you preach, it is best to acknowledge it, apologize and try to do better next time. Children will respect you for your honesty.

One way to be an inspiring parent and a positive role model is to be an expressive person, especially when it involves feelings. The younger the child, the more you should exaggerate. Have you ever seen a child excited? Children don't just look forward to things. They get excited, so excited that they can't stand it! Excitement and enthusiasm can be contagious. Let them catch your enthusiasm! When you're excited, you can raise your voice a notch, widen your eyes, and say, "Ooh, I am *sooo* excited we get to go to McDonald's to celebrate your birthday!"

In being a positive role model to young children, I like to make a big deal out of what I do. For example, I may slowly and intentionally share a bite of my ice cream and say, "Ooh, I just love sharing! It just makes me feel so good to share!"

I volunteer as an "angel" at my church. Angels help the Sunday school teachers. I usually help with the 3-year-olds and the 4-year-olds. When it's my turn to volunteer, I don't just assist the teachers by putting out the crayons on the table or by passing out the snacks. Instead, I model for the kids how I want them to behave in Sunday school.

When the teacher asks them who wants to help her pick up the crayons, I raise my hand high and enthusiastically say, "Oh, I do!" Then, I don't wait for the kids; I just start picking up the crayons. I tell the kids that I love to help others because it makes me feel so good. Then, I say, "Ooh, let's have a contest to see who can pick up the crayons faster." For some reason, they always manage to win!

When the teacher's about to read a book, I ask her to wait for me "because I don't want to miss anything." Then, I situate myself with the rest of the kids on the floor. I also lean forward and look intently at the teacher, as well as the book, and hope that the rest of the children will follow my lead. They usually make their way in front of me, so they can pay attention to the teacher.

With teenagers, all you have to do is practice what you preach. Another motivator is treating them as how they could be, rather than how they are sometimes. When I meet a teenager, I sometimes like to end our first session by saying, "You know, I can tell you are going to be somebody. I don't know what, but I can tell you're going to be somebody really, really important! And I know people! I'm a pretty good judge of character."

I say these things even if the child's dad tells me prior to the session that his child is having problems with stealing or lying or whatever. This is what I call "setting your child up for success." I haven't had too many teenagers argue with me using this approach...and they usually prove me right.

At a child's first appointment, I talk to her about the purpose and frequency of therapy, confidentiality, rules during the sessions, etc. One of the rules I have in therapy is that children under 13 cannot curse during the session. I allow some leeway for older teens to curse because cursing is so ingrained in them, it would be unrealistic for me to expect them to stop cursing all together. Although they may not use profanity in the home setting, they probably use it liberally with their peers. Still, I let them know that there's no cursing in therapy, unless it's to express their strong feelings, such as when they're writing a letter to the person who abused them. I explain to them that they can't indiscriminately say "f this" or "f that" during the sessions.

I also let them know that I expect them to respect me, just as I respect them. I inform them that there's no profanity allowed when it's used against other clients or me during the sessions. In all my years of working with children and teenagers, I only had one teenager, a 17-year-old, use profanity towards me. I told him, "I don't appreciate you calling me that. I made sure that I showed you the respect that you deserve, and I expect the same." During our next session, he apologized and we processed about what happened.

Summary:

- Encourage children to make responsible choices by acknowledging them and by praising them when they engage in positive behaviors.

- Encourage children by showing affection, as you praise them.
- Motivate children to monitor their own behaviors by maintaining a strong bond with them.
- Motivate children by teaching them about the different virtues in life through positive role modeling.
- Motivate them by allowing them to see themselves in a positive light and by letting them know that you expect great things from them.

Building Character

In working with children, I try to do more than change their behavior. My ultimate goal is to mold their character. However, I don't attempt a personality overhaul, nor do I try to change the essence of who they are. I believe that all children are essentially good by nature. Through socialization or environmental conditions, I believe they learn to act against the social norm. Therefore, I try to help them develop character through re-socialization.

I allow my clients to express their positive nature by providing a safe environment for them. Some may argue that in therapy, it's easier to affect a child's behavior because it's a controlled environment. However, even outside of the controlled setting, we can help to bring about positive behavioral changes in children.

You can control and influence your child's environment to some degree, at least in the home setting, by providing a place where they can feel safe and understood. Years ago, I wrote a mission statement in which I made a promise to help children be "healthy, happy and safe." It was a simple statement, but it still guides me to this day. In order for me to help children be emotionally and mentally healthy, I realized that I needed to go beyond teaching them simple behaviors. I want to teach them about things they can take to heart, to teach them that it's good to help others, to feel compassion for others and to respect and accept others.

I value each child's individuality. However, there are some characteristics that I value more than others in any individual.

In social work, we are taught to refrain from judging others. But, I believe, as a human being, I have to be honest and admit that there are some people that I just don't care to be around, and it's usually because of what I judge to be a character flaw in the individual.

However, there's good news! Character can be taught. I believe this with an unfaltering conviction because I've seen it happen. And I've been privileged to be a part of the learning process many times and with numerous children.

When I say character-building, I'm talking about building virtues and values, such as good work ethic, competitiveness, fairness, honesty, helpfulness, altruism, gentleness, kindness, empathy and so on. I try to help them develop compassion, love and concern for others, as well as patience, faith, perseverance and conscience.

You can teach children these qualities through modeling, role-playing and by praising them. With younger children you may also reward them when they show kindness toward another child or when they're helpful (refer to "Using Rewards and Privileges" under Chapter 5). You can also teach these qualities vicariously through books or by praising other children, in the child's presence.

One of the ways in which I learned to develop these qualities was by reading books on Abraham Lincoln, Thomas Jefferson and Eleanor Roosevelt. You can help children by having them read about such positive role models. Or, better yet, you can be their role model, here and now.

Teaching Kids Empathy, Sensitivity and Compassion

I believe much of children's problems can be resolved by helping them to develop empathy and compassion for others. It can address many of the problems they have with their friends, family members or society at large.

By teaching kids to be empathic and compassionate, I've helped children with major behavioral problems. By teaching them to have empathy for others, I've helped children who have sexually abused other children and those who have been cruel towards animals.

Several years ago, I heard an expert give a speech about her experience with sexual perpetrators. She indicated that true rehabilitation for the perpetrators couldn't occur without developing empathy for the victims. I believe this is the case.

When working with children who have sexually perpetrated others in the past, I can usually help them to stop their overt behaviors within a relatively short time. However, in most instances, I can tell by listening to what they have to say and by observing their subtle behaviors that they haven't internalized what's wrong and what's right.

Helping them to develop empathy takes a long, long time. Unless this is achieved, I believe that therapists do nothing more than postpone these children's intention to perpetrate again.

As discussed earlier, the best way to teach kids about these virtues is through modeling. During the session, I talk about these things directly with my clients. I define the words for them, and I give examples of each virtue. I let them know that it's good to develop these virtues. But, most importantly, I model these qualities for them. To make sure they understand these concepts, I also ask them to role-play these virtues using different scenarios.

Some may argue that I may be teaching them to mimic these virtues without actually internalizing them and this may be a possibility. However, it has been my experience that although they may be mimicking in the beginning, that with constant praises and recognition, children will ultimately internalize these virtues. It may be more difficult with teenagers, but I still make an effort to model these qualities for them, with the hope that my clients will internalize them one day.

Chapter 5

Using Natural and Logical Consequences

The most effective parenting skill involves learning to use natural and logical consequences. Using natural consequences means letting consequences happen naturally. For example, if your child goes outside without a raincoat, he'll get soaked. Logical consequences have to do with following through with consequences that are logical to the problem at hand. For instance, if your child runs down the aisles at the grocery store, she'll end up sitting in the shopping cart.

A word of warning: Please do not make promises if you don't intend to keep them. This goes for both rewards and consequences. Remember to follow through on what you say. Not following through with what you say is one of the biggest mistakes you can make as a parent.

When parents make threats based on their emotional reactions, they are probably not in a logical state of mind, and it's difficult to come up with logical consequences in this state of mind. Therefore, before responding to a child's misbehavior, take a moment to think about what would make sense in the given situation.

Example

Seven-year-old Maria has a fight with her 9-year-old brother, Allen, over which shows to watch on TV. Their mother, Joan feels frustrated and wants to give them a time-out. However, she remembers to take a moment to think of a logical consequence. Joan says casually, "I see you guys are having problems deciding what to watch on TV. Turn the TV off, and think of something else to do for the next 30 minutes. Don't worry, you'll have another chance to watch the TV together after awhile."

Maria and Allen try to argue with Joan. Joan remains calm and says, "If neither of you want to turn the TV off, I can turn it off myself. But that means I have to be the one to turn it back on. And I may not get around to turning it back on until you guys go to bed." Joan has given them a choice and has informed them of the possible consequences.

Joan's example is easier said than done. I know this because I find it difficult to keep my cool sometimes, and I teach these skills.

When I see a new client, I often feel like I'm being tested to see whether or not I can keep my emotions under control, and, more importantly, whether or not I can keep my reactions under control.

Sometimes, I just want to tell the children what to do and what not to do. And I want them to listen to me...and right now! I don't want to have to repeat myself or think about what I should do in a situation, especially if I'm having a rough day. But I eventually remember to take the time to think about what motivates this child to test his limits and what is causing him to act out. If I can understand the child' motivations, it's easier for me to come up with logical consequences that will get to the heart of the problem. If I get to the root cause of his problematic behavior, I can go a step beyond simply taking care of the superficial symptoms, which may find their way back to the surface after our session is done.

Example

Janice picks up her 5-year-old Lisa from daycare. The two of them make it home through rush hour traffic, and Janice gives

Lisa her snack. Finally, it's time for the best part of the day, their playtime together.

However, Lisa seems unhappy no matter what Janice suggests. Lisa decides to have a little tantrum and throws the board game halfway across the room. By now, Janice is getting frustrated and a little impatient. But Janice takes a moment, then says, "Lisa, you don't look too happy right now. What happened today?"

Lisa tells Janice that there was a new kid at daycare and that he tried to run outside when he wasn't supposed to. And he tried to bite the other kids and the teacher. Janice finds out that with all the chaos, nobody got to take a nap.

So, instead of giving Lisa a time-out or telling her that she can't play with the board game, Janice validates Lisa's frustration. "I see why you're not feeling too happy right now. It looks like you had a hard day." Then, as a logical consequence, Janice tells her, "Lisa, you can pick up the game pieces and put them back in the box. After you get done, you can go take a little nap, and maybe we can play later."

If Lisa says, "But I don't want to take a nap," Janice can tell her, "Okay. You don't have to. You can just go rest in your room for awhile and I'll come get you in a little bit to see if you feel like playing then."

This approach is not intended as a punishment. Instead, Janice is taking into account the cause or the motivation behind Lisa's misbehavior in giving out consequences that are fair and reasonable to the situation.

It takes time, effort and some creativity to come up with logical consequences. But it can make your life so much easier. Once you experience its magic, you'll want to use this approach again and again.

It was difficult for me to use this technique initially. For some reason, I just couldn't get the *logical* connection. When I first learned about logical consequences, I thought, "This is great. Now, I have something else I can use with my clients." But, I still relied on my old ways of doing things. I was still stuck in the "punishment routine," and I continued to *react* to my young clients based on my emotional reaction to their misbehaviors. It felt "unnatural" to respond to their behavior in a logical, rational fashion.

Then I finally grasped the concept. All I had to do was follow through with what makes sense in a given situation. Does the consequence relate to the inappropriate behavior? Would it help my client understand the connection between his misbehavior and the consequence? Would he realize, "If I lie, then I lose Ms. Kim's trust?" Or, "If I keep on telling her the truth from now on, then I can earn her trust back?"

I learned to follow through with this method over time. I also learned that I didn't have to get upset or take things personally when my clients decided to misbehave. One of the most important things I realized about using this technique was that I could respond to my clients matter-of-factly. I can be loving and accepting when I follow through with logical consequences by letting them know that they'll have another chance to make a better choice next time.

So, before lashing out with threats or punishments, let's take a minute to come up with a logical consequence. Does the consequence make sense, and does it relate to the problem? If not, think of something else.

Be creative in your approach to parenting, and be creative in coming up with logical consequences. Some may argue that there is a right way or a wrong way to parent children, and there may well be. But ultimately, what is important is what proves to be effective. If this approach proves to be successful in teaching children that they have choices, that they have the power to direct their lives and that they're accountable for their actions, then consider this the most effective parenting tool you will ever use.

Using logical consequences teaches children about choices and responsibilities (refer to "About Choices and Responsibility"). As they mature, you can let them come up with consequences, as well as rewards. If you are letting your teenager borrow the car for the evening, you could say, "If something happens, and you don't make it home by 10:30 this evening, what do you think we should do?" Hopefully, he'll come up with something that's fair and logical.

However, if his suggestions turn out to be a little self-serving, don't be surprised. Point out why his response isn't logical and then give him some examples of logical consequences for the issue at hand. He could lose the privilege of borrowing the car for a couple of days; he could lose the privilege of going out on weeknights, etc. The most important thing to remember in teaching him about responsibility is that the consequences must relate to the problem in some way. In other words, the consequences must be *logical*.

Whereas logical consequences require you to take time and energy, *natural consequences* require no effort on anyone's part. That is, it requires no effort on your part to *come up* with natural consequences. Nature assumes that responsibility. Unfortunately, that's not the hard part.

The hardest thing for a parent to do is watch his child suffer the natural consequence for her actions. It's very difficult for a parent to allow his teenager to run away from home and go hungry out on the streets. It's also difficult for a parent to let his 6-year-old go out barefooted before his child rushes back inside because of the snow.

But, sometimes, parents have no alternative but to rely on natural consequences. What can a parent do for his 16-year-old who repeatedly tries to run away from home? He could send his child to a treatment center, or he could try to get the legal system involved. But what if these measures fail? He can't keep his child locked up forever to shield her from the world. At some point, parents have to let go and let their children learn about life the only way their children know how.

Summary:

- Logical consequences allow children to learn from their choices.

- Logical consequences have to make sense, and they should relate to the problem in some way.

- Follow through with logical consequences on a consistent basis.

- Don't argue with children about logical consequences. Respect their choices by matter-of-factly following through with logical consequences.
- Keep your emotions in check and be as objective as possible.
- This technique should not be used as a punishment.
- Logical consequences should take into account the root causes of the problematic behaviors.
- Logical consequences should be fair and reasonable to the situation.
- In using this approach, it's important to respond to your child's misbehavior objectively, rather than react to his behavior based on your immediate emotional reaction.
- Be loving towards your children as you carry out logical consequences, and remind them that they have another chance to make a better choice next time.
- Logical consequences teach children about responsibility.
- Children can learn from natural consequences.
- In allowing your child to learn from natural consequences, try to refrain from rescuing him; allow your child to learn from his mistakes or choices.
- Natural consequences can be very effective in working with teenagers.

About Choices and Responsibility

Children need to have a choice to be responsible or irresponsible. Responsibility can not exist without freedom, and freedom, as I'm fond of telling my teenage clients, can not exist without responsibility.

With younger children, it's probably a good idea to limit their choices. As they grow older, they can cope with more than two choices without getting too overwhelmed or distracted. A child can have choices regarding household rules, chores, or anything else that are appropriate for his level of functioning.

Example

Jason, a 16 year-old, wants to go to the movies with his friends. His father, Pete might say, "Jason, you better be home from the movies by 10:00 p.m., or else you'll be grounded."

In contrast, Pete could say, "Well, Jason, today is Thursday. What do you think is a reasonable time for you to come home this evening?" In this instance, Jason has a choice and, more importantly, he has a choice to be responsible or irresponsible. Pete has given Jason a choice in coming up with a reasonable time for him to return home.

If Jason agrees to 10:00 p.m., then there is no problem. However, if he wants to go out with his friends after the movie, then Pete and Jason have more negotiating to do. During the negotiation Pete could say, "How about coming home by 10:00 or 10:30, since it's a school night? And you can stay out later tomorrow or Saturday evening." Either time Jason chooses Pete will probably be happy with since he could live with either one.

However, if Jason refuses to accept 10:00 or 10:30, then Pete can tell him that he can stay in for the evening but remind Jason that he could still stay out late on the weekend. At this point Jason will probably agree to come home by 10:30 p.m.

If for any reason Jason fails to come home by the set time, Pete does not have to resort to lecturing him. Instead, he can inform Jason that he may not go out on weeknights, at least for the next two weeks, until he is able to make more responsible choices.

Setting Limits Regarding
Rules and Boundaries

Children need to learn about limits and boundaries, just as they need to learn about choices and responsibilities (later in the book, I'll talk about respecting personal boundaries and sexual boundaries). When I first heard that children actually want grown-ups to set limits for them, I thought my boss was crazy.

But she taught me that although children may argue with grown-ups about rules, they actually feel safer with the rules in place. Boundaries let children know that there is a limit to what you would allow them to do in order to keep them safe.

It has been my experience that without the rules being concretely spelled out for them, children feel that they have to test the limits to see just how far they can go before they're told they can't do something. Until the bounds are made clear, I believe that some children actually feel anxious and try to have the adults around them clearly establish limits.

Case Study

Melissa went over to a friend's house with her child for the first time. Her son, Raymond suddenly felt compelled to act out while she was talking to her friend. Melissa and I analyzed the situation in order to prevent this behavior from happening again. First of all, Raymond was in a different setting. He did not know what the limits were in the new environment. Secondly, he wasn't sure who was in charge. Instead of turning to his mother he decided to "act out" in order to have his boundaries set for him in the new setting.

To avoid this situation, go over the rules with your child prior to leaving your home, whether you are going to a friend's house or to a new restaurant. This is especially important in order to prevent your child from taking control over the situation. Have a strategy and, as always, remember to be brief and to the point in order to be effective in your approach.

You could say, "Hey, my friend has a son who's about your age. Ooh, I think you guys will get along just great! You can play with him all you want while we're there. The rules at his house are the same as here. There's no running around the house, but you can play with his toys if he lets you. You can watch cartoons with him, but not the movie channel."

One of the parents whom I interviewed for this book reminded me to "save the *no's* for the big things, especially with teenagers." If you constantly tell young people "no," they're bound to become frustrated. Worse still, they may decide to redefine to word entirely. "No" could come to mean, "maybe" or "yes, as long as I don't get caught."

If parents insist on saying "no" most of the time, this may motivate children to do what they want, regardless of the possible consequences. When they get to this point, it's very difficult to re-establish your authority. Remember to say "yes" as often as possible. If you have to say "no," tell them what they can do instead. For instance, you can say, "Don't play on Mommy's computer, John, but you can play with the Play Station."

Children naturally need the freedom to grow and to learn from their mistakes…and bad choices. With younger children, it's okay to be more direct or leading in your attempt to encourage them to make better choices.

With teenagers you may have to respect their choices even if you disagree with them. Teens may do exactly the opposite of what you tell them to do. Even if they know you are right. This is because they're going through a stage in which they're struggling with developing their own identity and they feel a need assert their independence by disagreeing with adults. Remember to give teenagers more leeway and the freedom they need to learn from their mistakes, as long as their lives are not in jeopardy.

You can set geographical boundaries for children as well. They should know, in advance, how far they can wonder off from the house. "You can play in the backyard so I can watch you from the window." Or, "Don't play out in the street. But you can play in the driveway." As children mature and prove themselves to be more responsible, you can extend their boundaries.

Example

Jimmy is a 16-year-old teenager who just received his driver's license a week ago. His mother, Mary, wants to support him in his efforts to be as self-sufficient as possible. He's currently working at a fast food restaurant so he can save enough money to buy his first car.

It usually takes Jimmy 20 minutes on his bike to get to work. Mary could say, "Jimmy, you can take my car to work today. It looks like it's going to rain." She can add with a smile, "But don't get lost and end up in downtown. Please bring my baby back home straight from work." Jimmy will probably roll his eyes but still agree to her terms. At which point, Mary can add with a wink, "I'm talking about the car."

Ouch! But for some reason, teens seem to respond to such approaches. It's short, simple, funny and, most importantly, it's not a lecture!

Summary:

- Children need clear limits and boundaries in order to feel secure.
- Tell them what they can do and not just what they can't do.
- Let them learn from their choices, even if you disagree with their choices (as long as their choices do not endanger their lives).
- With teenagers, be matter-of-fact in your approach and respect their choices, whether positive or negative.

Using Rewards and Privileges

A reward system can be highly effective in shaping children's behavior. There are guidelines you can follow to get the most out of using rewards. First of all, make sure the reward is appropriate for the child's age.

One of the most important, and often overlooked, considerations is whether or not a child likes the reward. The reward won't be as effective if it isn't important to the child. Remember, what you like is not necessarily what a child likes.

The younger the child, the quicker the reward. This is because their attention span is shorter, and they may not get the connection otherwise.

Additionally, the reward doesn't have to be expensive. It can start out as a sticker, a checkmark or a smiley face. I remember when I was in elementary school and how I used to live for those smiley faces on my tests and homework.

In therapy, candy has a special meaning. With candy, I can nurture my clients, as I reward them for helping me clean up at the end of the session. It's a way for me to bond with them (I make a point to explain to them in the initial session that they can have a piece of candy with their parents' permission. I ask the parents so that the children learn they shouldn't accept candy from anyone without their parents' permission).

I also explain to them that they can get a piece of candy if they help clean up the toys at the end of the session. However, I clarify for them that we have a special rule in therapy; they don't have to clean up if they don't want to. I point out that this rule is probably different from the rules at home. I explain to them that we have a different rule because therapy is special.

I let them know, "If you don't feel like cleaning up, all you have to say is that you don't feel like cleaning up and you don't feel like getting a piece of candy today." In my entire career as a therapist, I had only two clients who tested me on this, before they learned they could trust me to keep my word.

With these two children, I restrained myself from repeatedly reminding them to clean up, and I did not beg them to help me. At the end of the session, I told them that it was time to clean up. When they continued to play, I asked them if they wanted to help me clean up today. One of them said he didn't want to, and the other chose not to respond at all.

I finished cleaning up the toys and got up to leave the session. Naturally, they asked me about the candy. I matter-of-factly asked them what they thought I should do. Neither expected me to give them the candy. I assured them they would still have another chance to get a piece of candy after the next session. I left it at that, and the children did not argue with me.

The goal is to wean children off material rewards as they mature by replacing concrete rewards with "social rewards." You can help them internalize appropriate behaviors by praising them and by helping them to monitor and guide their own behaviors.

A reward system can be gradual. For example, you can give 5-year-old Eddie a star each time he cleans his room, brushes his teeth, and so on. If he gets five stars by the end of the day, he can pick a toy from the special "Toy Jar" (toys that cost 25 cents or less) before his bedtime.

It is a good idea to give the reward at least an hour before his bedtime so he'll have a chance to benefit from the reward. How would you feel if your boss told you that you had to wait a week to cash your paycheck?

Remember to follow through with your promises. It is just as damaging to your credibility to make empty promises as it is to give out empty threats. If you don't follow through, your child will learn not to believe you the next time that you make promises.

Privileges could be used in a similar way. A child's age is especially important in this case. One privilege may not be appropriate for both a 5-year-old and a 12-year-old. You can keep track of their behaviors in earning their privileges the same way as you track their behavior for the rewards.

Summary:

- Using a reward system can be highly effective in influencing a child's behavior.
- Rewards and privileges should be age-appropriate and your child should like them.
- The younger the child, the quicker the reward.
- Restrain from repeatedly reminding your child about the reward.
- Wean children off the material rewards and replace them with social rewards (or praises).
- Be consistent in following through with rewards or privileges.

About Using Corporal Punishment and Time-outs

I put using time-outs under the same heading as corporal punishment because it is a form of punishment. Initially, I did not realize this and used time-outs rather freely, until a coworker told me that I should use this technique as a last resort. It was easy to use and made my life easier. But, over time, I learned that by relying on time-outs, I wasn't allowing children to learn from their mistakes.

Time-outs can be effective in stopping the immediate unwanted behavior, but this technique can prove to be ineffective in the long run, unless you are able to supervise your children constantly. Time-outs fail to control your children's behavior in your absence because they know they are free from immediate consequences. The objective is to teach them to maintain their own behavior without any supervision. Therefore, it is better to rely on natural and logical consequences instead of time-outs.

I believe there are situations in which it may be appropriate for a parent to remove a child from a given situation. For instance, if 5-year-old Marcus insists on sitting in front of the TV screen blocking everyone's view, he can be excused from the living room for five minutes, to go to the designated time-out area. After five minutes, he'll have another opportunity to watch TV and allow others to enjoy it as well.

In deciding to use time-outs, there are several measures that should be taken to make this approach more effective in deterring unwanted behaviors. It is important that parents refrain from using time-outs indiscriminately, and, as discussed previously, it should be reserved as a last resort. As a "rule of thumb," a child should be given a minute of time-out for each year in age.

Example

Four-year-old Tommy spills a bowl of peanuts off of the coffee table because he was running around in the living room. His mom, Carol, could send him to a designated time-out area for four minutes. Tommy probably won't stay in time-out for an extended length of time anyway due to his lack of attention span.

Carol doesn't have to struggle with him about completing his time-out. It's a good idea to have a kitchen timer for this purpose. This prevents him from asking every thirty seconds, "Is my time up?"

If he does ask that question, Carol doesn't have to respond to him. She can let him know (before his time starts) that his time will be up when the timer rings. If Tommy insists on repeating the question, she can tell him that there will be extra time added to the time-out for each instance he asks the question.

Carol could have avoided all of this by using logical consequences instead. Immediately following the accident, she could have said, "Oops! The peanuts spilled." At this point some children will automatically pick up the peanuts and put them back into the bowl.

If Tommy doesn't get the hint, she can simply ask him to do so matter-of-factly. As a logical consequence, she could also add, "If you're having problems staying in the living room, you can go play in your room for a little while."

This may resemble time-outs, but it's not the same. Carol is merely giving him an option to change the location of where he would like to play or change his behavior while he remains in the living room. In this example, he can still choose to play in his room, whereas in a time-out he would not have the option to play.

Ideally, the time-out area should be away from the TV or any other pleasurable activities. Time-outs are ineffective with children over eight years of age, because they believe time-outs are stupid and insulting and they resent being treated like a child. Time-outs are also ineffective with children who are two years old or younger, because they typically don't understand the purpose of time-outs and because they lack the attention span to stay in a time-out.

Naturally, using time-outs is preferred to using corporal punishment. Personally and professionally, I do not use or endorse using corporal punishment, even though I realize that using corporal punishment is not the same thing as physically abusing a child.

The National Center on Child Abuse and Neglect defines physical abuse as "an act of commission by a parent or caretaker which is not accidental and...which results in physical injury" (Clark & Clark, 1989, p. 134). Physical abuse has to do with intentionally causing an injury to a child.

I've worked with many parents who believed in using corporal punishment. Some of these parents were court-mandated clients, whose children were removed from home by child protective agencies. These parents tried to use corporal punishment to teach their children. Although they did not intend to abuse their children, their use of corporal punishment often resulted in "fractures, burns, bruises, welts, cuts and/or internal injuries" (Clark & Clark, 1989, p. 134).

They were required to attend a certain number of sessions or classes, in which they had to learn about alternative approaches to parenting. They had to learn about disciplining their children without resorting to physical punishment, before they were allowed to reunite with their children.

During the sessions, these parents explained that they didn't intend to abuse their children. However, they usually admitted they probably weren't in a logical state of mind when they used corporal punishment on their children. They agreed they were emotionally *reacting* to their children, rather than rationally *responding* to their inappropriate behaviors.

Using corporal punishment can be dangerous and it has too many undesirable side effects. It can damage the relationship between a parent and her child. If you were to spank your child, she probably wouldn't feel the need to come up to you and tell you about what happened at school. You would probably get a nice dose of the silent treatment for at least a few minutes or hours, maybe longer.

Another negative side effect has to do with teaching children about violence. They may learn that it's okay to use physical aggression to get their way or to make their point, as long as they're bigger than the other guy. It also teaches them that it's okay to express their anger or frustration through physical aggression.

Summary:

- Time-outs are effective only under highly supervised and controlled situations.
- Time-outs are a form of punishment and should be reserved as a last resort.

- As a "rule of thumb," time-outs should be given one minute per each year of age.
- Use a timer to count down the time with younger children.
- Time-outs should be carried out away from the TV or any other pleasurable activities.
- Past the age of eight, time-outs tend to be ineffective.
- Some instances of corporal punishment can turn into child abuse, as defined by law.
- There are serious side effects to using corporal punishment. It damages the relationship with your children, and it endorses the use of violence.

Chapter 6

Teaching Children Age-Appropriate Social Skills

Many children in institutional settings, as well as those who have been severely neglected, lack age-appropriate social skills. I used to travel all over Texas to read children's records and interview children who were in the State's custody. These records indicated that at least 95% of them lacked age-appropriate social skills.

As we all know, social skills are very important if we want to survive in our society. Often, these children are behind the rest of the children in the general population in their level of social functioning. I recently read a journal article which indicated that although our nation's foster care system may teach children independent living skills, such as budgeting and interviewing skills, these children often have difficulty coping in our society, both socially and emotionally, once they are emancipated.

Some of these children suffer even more devastating effects. They are at an increased risk for unintended pregnancy, substance abuse and homelessness sometime during their life after being emancipated.

Case Study

I had a 14-year-old client, who was recently placed in a very loving foster home. It was obvious that he was behind his peers in social skills. He told me that he had younger friends and that his oldest friend was nine years old. I consulted with the foster parents and recommended that they encourage him to start playing with children who were closer to his age.

I suggested that they give him plenty of opportunity to "hang around" 12- or 13-year-olds who weren't too socially advanced for him. My client was developmentally delayed, and I did not want him to be subject to negative peer pressure where the older children might take advantage of him.

I recommended that he join the youth group at their church so that he could be around other teenagers in a positive environment. I also suggested that the foster parents encourage him to watch shows on television geared toward teenagers, rather than Saturday morning cartoons.

My client had problems relating to his 9-year-old friend, as well as other 14-year-olds. He told me that some of his peers at school made fun of him and called him names. So, I taught him to use assertive communication to speak up for himself, and we talked about ignoring or avoiding his negative peers.

We also read the book *Every Kid's Guide to Making Friends* by Joy Berry. We role-played various situations in which he could use the skills in the book to relate to his peers.

Involving Children during Problem-Solving

It is best to involve children during the problem-solving process. This increases the likelihood that they will follow through with the consequences. Having them involved in this process can actually decrease the likelihood of them having to serve any consequences at all.

Here's how this process works. Choose a "neutral time." That means do not disturb kids during their favorite TV shows. Choose a time that is open for everyone, like after dinner or a couple of hours before bedtime. Matter-of-factly talk to them about a certain problem they've been having lately. It's best not to begin the conversation with, "We need to talk," because that immediately puts them on the defensive.

Here's a sample dialogue.

Mom: *Jason, I know you've been pretty busy lately with football practice and the band. I know that you've been busy with your friends as well, but the last progress report you brought home had a couple of C's and a D on it. I really want to support you in your activities at school, and I know your friends are important to you. What do you think we can do so that you can keep up with your grades, your extracurricular activities, as well as your friends?*

Son: *I don't know.*

Mom: *You know, I really would like for us to figure something out, together. I know that your grades are pretty important to you. And they're pretty important to me too. Now, I can come up with suggestions, but I really want to know what you think we should do. I may not know about everything you have to do these days.*

Son: *How about if I just bring my grades up? I won't make any D's.*

Mom: *Okay, that's a good goal. How do you think you can do that?*

Son: *What if I finish my homework before I go out with my friends during the week?*

If Jason doesn't respond to his mother this way, his mother may have to make more suggestions to help him brainstorm about possible solutions. Problem solving requires that both parties participate in the brainstorming process to generate many different possibilities. The parent's role is to refrain from judging any of the child's suggestions during the brainstorming stage.

After this stage, they can plan for the implementation of the possible solutions. In the above example, Jason and his mom can narrow the list down to the top five or ten mutually agreed upon solutions. Then they can decide which solutions to try first.

They need to decide in advance what to do if one approach doesn't work. If Jason doesn't do what he agreed to do, then his mother can respect his choice and follow through with the consequence that they both agreed on during the problem-solving process. If he argues or complains about the consequence, she can firmly but matter-of-factly remind him that the outcome was his choice.

Summary:

- Involving children during the problem-solving process increases the likelihood that they'll agree to the logical consequences.

- Problem solving should take place during a neutral time.

- Brainstorm for several possible, creative solutions.

- After the brainstorming process, rule out unworkable, unfair or unrealistic solutions.

- Always have at least two backup solutions.

- Follow through consistently with the agreed upon solutions.

Increasing Your Child's Coping Skills

When you teach or encourage children to express their feelings, you're helping them develop what I believe to be one of the most important coping skills in managing their behavior. Just being able to express their feelings directly and openly, without the fear of having their feelings negated or minimized, helps them cope and withstand just about any problem that may come their way.

However, in some instances, children will need to do more than express their feelings in order to solve their problems. You can help increase their coping skills by including them in the problem-solving process. Teaching children to keep their cool under pressure can help them increase their coping skills as well.

One way I like to show that they have control over their emotions is by pointing out that they're able to restrain themselves in other situations. For instance, I may tell Bobby, "You were able to keep from punching the principal in the nose when you were mad at her. So if you can take half a second to decide not to hit the principal, that means you can take half a second to decide not to hit your sister."

Young people should also be encouraged to take on flexible roles. For example, you can teach girls that they can wear a dress but still play on the basketball team. They can help fix the car, and they can help you cook. You can teach boys that they can be emotionally strong but also turn to others for comfort when they need help.

Children may become stuck in unhealthy roles. They may think that they are *supposed* to be a certain way. For instance, if a child is used to being the "perfect child" in trying to rescue or please others, tell her that it's not her responsibility to constantly live for others. You can tell her that she can have her own needs, wants and preferences.

Through modeling, you can teach her to use assertive communication skills, so she can stand up for her rights or values. For instance, you can teach her to say, "No thanks. I don't drink." Or, "No. I like you a lot, but I don't want to have sex before marriage." Let her know that she doesn't need to make excuses for her choices and that she doesn't need to lie about her beliefs.

Chapter 7

Increasing Your Child's Self-Esteem

A child's state of mental health is closely related to his level of self-esteem. Some of the parenting books I've read suggest that parents restrain from personalizing their child's behavior, whether negative or positive.

I don't think there is anything wrong with this recommendation. However, I prefer to personalize the positive behaviors, while depersonalizing the negative behaviors. In other words, separate the behavior from the child when he engages in a negative behavior.

Instead of saying, "You're a bad boy!" when a child decides to hit another boy, you could say, "It's not okay to hit when you're angry. Tell him you're angry with words." In contrast, if your child brings home an 'A' or a 'B' on a spelling test, personalize it by saying, "You are such a smart boy! You are such a hard worker!"

Every so often, there is a child that may try to prove that her parents are wrong when they praise her in this way. It may be that she's going through a power struggle. In her case, an appropriate response may be, "You can think whatever you'd like. But I think you're great!"

Another way to increase children's self-esteem is by asking them for their help. It's very rare that a young child would refuse to help, especially if asked the right way. If a child refuses to help me, I accept her answer and move on. I may ask another child to help me instead. At this point, the first child usually changes her mind. She suddenly becomes highly motivated to help me and, in fact, may get into an argument with the second child about helping me. In this case, I find a way for both children to have the "privilege" of helping me.

Then, I make a big deal out of it! I tell them what good helpers they are, and how I don't know what I would do without them. Children love exaggerations! Exaggerations may even work with teenagers if you touch them up with a little humor. Although they know when you are being melodramatic, they may still appreciate your gratitude.

Case Study

Most of the young people I've worked with came to me with very low self-esteem and poor self-image. For instance, a few years ago, I worked with a teenager who used to live in a gang-infested neighborhood. Sam was placed in a foster home in a very rural area.

When I first met him, he told me that he wanted to be a bum and that he wanted to sleep and smoke pot all day. I didn't respond to him initially and I didn't appear shocked. I didn't laugh or respond in any way he might have found reinforcing. I just let him go on talking.

Towards the end of the session, I matter-of-factly told Sam that no matter what he thought of himself, that I thought he was going to grow up to be somebody. I said, "I don't think you know just how capable you are."

"You tell me that you want to be a bum, and all you want to do is sleep and smoke pot all day. But I don't buy that. I'm not sure exactly what you're going to do when you grow up, but I have a feeling that you're going to be somebody special."

Sam looked surprised, but he didn't argue with me. He may never have thought of himself as anything more than a bum or a gang member. It's possible no one has ever helped him to see that he could be somebody. I was convinced that he could become someone other than a bum or a gang member or a drug addict. I believe I gave him something to think about that day, and I helped him to see that there were other possibilities for him.

About five months later, when he was planning for his graduation from high school, Sam told me that he wanted to be a veterinarian assistant. He had problems saying the word, "veterinarian," but I told him that I thought he would make a great veterinarian assistant!

Case Study

Another client of mine started improving his behaviors as quickly as one month after I started seeing him. His foster parents were extremely skilled as parents, and I believe much of his improvement had to do with the way they related to him.

During one of our family sessions, my client proudly announced that he was getting better. His foster parents and I agreed with him and praised him. I also told him, "And you better get used to it, because I think you're going to keep on getting better and better."

He told me he felt "weird" when people praise him. I validated and normalized his feelings. I told him, "It's okay to feel uncomfortable. But you can keep on getting better anyway. It sure beats getting into trouble, doesn't it?" He smiled and agreed with me.

Summary:

- In helping children increase their self-esteem, personalize the positive behaviors and depersonalize the negative behaviors.
- Ask them to help you and let them know how much you appreciate them.
- Exaggeration and humor can be injected into praises.
- Praises can help children see themselves in a new, positive light.

The Importance of Showing Affection

Children who lack physical affection in the home are more likely than their counterpart to have sex at an earlier age. Perhaps, it's because sex involves touching, whether it's intimate or not.

Fortunately, children do not have to engage in sex to be touched positively. As your child's parent or caregiver, you may provide her with the touch that she needs so desperately. You may give her positive touches by petting her on the head, her back or her shoulder, as you praise her. You can hold her hand or let her lean against you for comfort. If she's three or four years old, you can let her sit on your lap if the situation is appropriate.

If you're a foster parent or an adoptive parent, you may be worried about your child possibly misinterpreting your touches or, worse yet, making false allegations of sexual abuse. In the general public there is, at most, four to ten percent false allegations. Having worked with numerous foster children in various foster homes, I know that the statistics for false allegations for both physical and sexual abuse is higher in these settings.

However, you can rest a little easier because there are steps you can take to avoid serious complications caused by false allegations:

- Show children physical affection in front of others.
- Talk to them about different touches—good touches, bad touches and secret touches (to be discussed further in the chapter regarding sexually abused children).
- Have an open family meeting, where you and your children can talk about touching, as well as maintaining appropriate boundaries.
- Teach children that touching should never be a secret when it involves them.
- Demonstrate for them how they can touch others appropriately. For example, pat them on the back, hold their hand or give them a "side hug."
- Let children know that they deserve "good touches" and "good hugs."

Example

A few months ago, I talked to a friend of mine about her strained relationship with her teenage son. She thought that since he was getting older, he probably didn't want to be touched as much as he did when he was a younger kid. This didn't occur to her on a conscious level, but she started cutting down on her physical affection towards him.

I suggested that she go back to giving him more positive touches, like patting him on the back or playfully punching him on the arm. I also suggested that she praise him often. She told me a couple of weeks later how her relationship with her son had improved drastically since she started showing him more physical affection. She said she wasn't sure if the praises made as much difference as the touching. In either case, she said that their relationship was better and that they were actually communicating with each other.

Example

One day, a good friend of mine told me that his mom said she loved him. I thought it was nice, but I couldn't understand why he was so excited.

My friend explained to me that neither of his parents had ever told him that they loved him. He said he was sure that they loved him by their actions but that "those" words were never spoken in his family. His mother finally decided to tell him because she was about to go overseas on a long vacation. He said, "I guess she was scared something might happen to her while she was on vacation."

I asked him about his response. He said, "I told her I loved her right back. Just like that." He told me that he usually doesn't know how to respond when people catch him off guard like that. He said it felt "really good" to hear his mom say those words, and that he was glad he was able to tell her that he loved her as well. They still don't exchange those words too often, but considering that my friend was in his 30's before they ever said "I love you" to each other, it was a giant step forward.

My friend still hasn't told his dad that he loves him or vice versa. I suggested that he try telling his dad indirectly. One day my friend called his mother, and his father happened to be in the same room as her. Before he hung up the phone, my friend told his mom that he loved her and said, "And tell Dad I love him too." A few seconds later, my friend's mom said, "Dad wants me to tell you that he loves you too." That was good enough for my friend.

If you love your children, please tell them that you love them. It's important for you to show them that you love them, but it's equally important for them to hear those words.

Involving Children in Extra-Curricular Activities

Studies indicate that children who participate in extra curricular activities tend to make higher grades than those who are not involved in such activities. The higher grades may have to do with their level of responsibility, their ability to learn time management skills or their self-esteem. Whatever the reason, children tend to make better grades when they have other responsibilities outside of academics.

There are many ways to get your children involved in activities and in the community. Volunteering at a local nursing home or at an animal shelter is a great way for children to be involved. Not only does it help them perform better in school, their involvement can help others, which is a great boost for their self-esteem.

Chapter 8

Additional Parenting Techniques

Using Distractions

One of my favorite techniques in parenting is to use distractions. This approach works especially well with younger children. Sometimes, children are too sophisticated to respond to this technique. However, even with teenagers, distractions can be effective in redirecting their behavior, if used creatively. When observing your children initiating something inappropriate, you can intervene immediately, without directly addressing the problematic behavior.

For example, if 6-year-old Tommy insists on a toy when they pass by the toy isle at the grocery store, his mom can become completely melodramatic to catch him off-guard. She could say, "Oh my gosh, Tommy, I almost forgot the cheese for the nachos we're having tonight!" As she quickly steers the cart towards the cheese aisle, she could say, "Tommy, do you remember the special cheese you liked on your nachos the last time we had them? Could you please help me find the right kind?" Change the subject. It usually works!

Countering the Effects of Boredom

Boredom is one of the greatest enemies for children and teenagers. Boredom can lead to lower grades, lack of motivation and even delinquency. When children don't have social outlets that they find meaningful or enjoyable, they turn elsewhere to fill in the gap in their lives. This often leads them to join gangs, engage in vandalism or other delinquent activities.

Making bad grades is not as bad as shooting someone. Still, most parents want their children to make good grades. A possible solution to their boredom, and possibly their bad grades, is to encourage them or get them to be involved in organized activities while they're still young.

For instance, for younger children, you can involve them in the Boy Scouts or the Girl Scouts. For older children, you can encourage them to be active in school or community sports, church activities, or even volunteer organizations. Some teenagers counter the effects of boredom by getting a job. Not only does this help them with their boredom, but it also comes in handy when they get ready to buy their first car.

When children are bored at school, it's a little more challenging. Although you can't tell the teachers to be a little more exciting during the class, you can help your child by maintaining a good working relationship with his teachers.

With a little bit of diplomacy and a friendly attitude, you can go a long way with them. "I'm so glad Tommy's in your class! It's so good to have new teachers come to our school. It's almost like our kids have a fresh start! If there's anything I can do to help out with Tommy or if there is anything else I can do, please don't hesitate to call me."

They may pay a little more attention to your child because of the contact. You can let your younger children know about the meetings with their teachers. This tends to keep some children a little more alert during the class.

However, if you are dealing with a teenager, you have to play it cool, especially around his friends. You can matter-of-factly explain to him that you are not trying to spy on him and that you're trying to be actively involved as a parent because you understand the importance of school. Then, you can negotiate with him about when it would be appropriate for you to have contact with his teachers.

With younger children, you can make school work a little bit more exciting by having them participate in a "contest." "Ooh! Becky, Why don't you have a contest to see how many more vocabulary words you can learn today compared to yesterday? I bet you'll be surprised!" You can also set up a reward system for her, in which she can trade in her achievements for a reward.

With older children, you can acknowledge their accomplishments and their hard work. They may respond to your praises, or they may prefer privileges or rewards. You should be generous in either case, but you should also remind them that in the end their hard work is for their benefit.

Having Fun with Your Child

The most important rule is to have fun. Sometimes adults forget this when playing with children. Recreational activities turn into lectures, instead of an opportunity to have fun with children and to bond with them.

The activity should be age-appropriate. Also, you should refrain from correcting or criticizing them during your special time together, unless there is potential for harm (for example, if your child tries to "show off" by jumping off the top of the slide, it would be appropriate for you to correct her behavior).

You should try to let them have control during play. This allows them to get their control needs met in an appropriate setting. It also stimulates their creativity. If your purpose is to teach them about some of the realities in life, you can take turns making up the rules (such as when the two of you are playing cards).

The activity should be child-centered as much as possible, when trying to build rapport with children. That means they should be interested in the activity, and they should have a voice in choosing the activity (unless it's a surprise!).

Having fun doesn't have to be expensive or time-consuming. What's important is that you interact with them as much as possible. You can have planned "family fun time," and you can also have a planned special time with each of your children. A family doesn't have to do everything together in order to be a healthy family. In fact, that's not healthy! That's an *enmeshed* family, that is, a family in which individuality is discouraged.

For bonding purposes it is better to engage in more interactive activities. For instance, playing tennis or chess with your child does more for rapport building than watching the television together.

Each member should take turns choosing the activity. Most importantly, parents need to follow through with their plans. There's nothing worse than having a child look forward to an activity and then being let down because his parents are too busy.

How to Have a Family Meeting

Family meetings can be a great time for your family members to bond with each other. During the meetings, you should try to include all of the members for consistency. There may be times when some of them should be excluded due to the inappropriate subject matter. For example, you wouldn't want to involve your 5-year-old when talking about your 16-year-old's drug use.

Both parents should attend the meetings for consistency, as well as unity. Parents should agree or compromise on the issue prior to the meetings, and ground rules should be covered in advance, such as no cursing, no name-calling, no blaming and no criticizing.

You should inform all relevant family members in advance of the time and place of the meeting. There are times when the subject matter should be brought up at the meeting itself, such as when the subject is your teen's alcohol use. You don't want her to come up with any brilliant excuses while she's in school.

Family meetings should not take place at the dinner table. Dinner should be a pleasant time, and confrontation should be minimized while eating. A regular family meeting at a regular, set schedule can prevent conflict between family members, as well as prevent future problems regarding household chores, rules, etc.

You can have your teenagers sign a contract if the issue is significant. In doing this, you can use the problem-solving approach. Most importantly, family meetings can be about fun things, like planing a trip, preparing for a picnic, etc.

Part Two
Therapeutic Parenting Skills

A Word of Warning

The symptoms for all the problem areas listed in this part of the book are based largely on *Diagnostic and Statistical Manual of Mental Disorders-Fourth Edition* (DSM-IV), a reference book on various emotional and mental disorders. **Please note that if your child has just one or two of the symptoms under a disorder, it probably does not indicate that your child has the disorder. Instead, your child must display several or most of the symptoms for a specified length of time in order to meet the criteria for a particular disorder or a problem.**

You may observe the same symptom under several of the problem areas. For instance, if a 6-year-old child has nightmares, it doesn't necessarily indicate that he was sexually abused. It could mean he's anxious about starting school or that he's depressed about his parents' divorce. Even if he tries to touch another child's private parts, it doesn't automatically signal abuse. It could mean that he's going through a normal developmental stage in which children try to explore the differences between girls and boys.

I strongly advise parents to refrain from making the diagnosis at home. The symptoms listed herein are intended to serve as a guideline to determine whether or not it would be in your child's best interest for you to take your child to a professional therapist, psychologist, psychiatrist or medical doctor for a thorough evaluation and/or an intervention.

Lastly, a child does not have to display all of the symptoms in any particular problem area in order to benefit from the therapeutic parenting skills outlined under each of the problem areas. I have included case studies to illustrate these skills and you can apply these skills successfully even if your child exhibits one or just a few of the symptoms listed under a particular area.

Chapter 9

Attention-Deficit/Hyperactivity Disorder (ADHD) and Oppositional Behaviors

---

The following are possible signs and symptoms of ADHD:

- Hyperactivity or excessive movement (for example, difficulty remaining in his/her seat during class)
- Unable to focus on tasks or complete tasks
- Easily distracted
- Difficulty completing sentences before skipping onto another subject
- Repeated school referrals for behavioral or academic problems
- Excessive tardiness
- Often forgetful
- Frequently disruptive in social situations or in the classroom setting

Based on my experience, I believe ADHD is usually not an isolated disorder. Most of my clients with this problem had other diagnoses as well. ADHD is often related to sexual or physical abuse of a child or neglect of a child. However, it should be noted that not all children who have been abused have this problem. Some children whose parents recently separated or divorced may show some symptoms of ADHD.

Research indicates that a combination of medication and parenting skills training is one of the most effective approaches to working with children with ADHD. As with any childhood behavioral or emotional problem, I do not indiscriminately recommend that the child be assessed for possible medication. I usually recommend such evaluation only when a child has severe symptoms or when there seems to be an organic or hereditary basis for the problem.

Psychiatrists often change the dosages of medications due to the side effects or due to the ineffectiveness of the child's current dosage. I can usually tell when the child's medication has been changed, without being first informed by the parents.

With some children, medication may be effective in managing their emotional or behavioral problems, at least partially. Medication can also help with their social interactions and their school performance. However, without behavioral or other interventions, such as parenting skills training or family therapy, it's difficult to treat children with ADHD on a long-term basis.

Children who have problems with oppositional behaviors may exhibit the following symptoms:

- Overtly defiant regarding household or classroom rules
- Passively defiant (the child agrees to complete a task but intentionally fails to carry it out)
- Excessively argumentative
- Has tantrums
- Has difficulty taking responsibility for his/her actions
- Is easily angered
- Has difficulty with school performance
- Has difficulty socially (making or keeping friends)

Inattentiveness and Hyperactivity

Children with ADHD or oppositional problems tend to respond well to natural and logical consequences. It's important to limit their choices, especially when parenting children with ADHD. They can become easily frustrated when faced with more than two choices because they may become overwhelmed thinking about the different choices. You can cut down on their confusion by simplifying their choices, as in, "You can study for an hour now and then for another hour after dinner, or you can study for two hours now."

In some instances, you can help children by blocking out distractions in their environment. For example, you can put up cardboard barriers between them and their siblings during study time.

This method is effective in helping children who have difficulty maintaining their focus. You can use a similar approach by having them go to a designated study area. It's almost impossible to have your child do her homework in the living room, with the TV on, surrounded by other family members.

It may prove to be more effective if you tell her that she has one hour to complete the homework in her room (the TV should be removed from her room, and the toys should stay in the playroom or the living room where you can monitor their use). You can also remind her that she's free to watch the TV in the living room after she completes her assignment.

You can tell her that you are willing to help her by checking her homework *after* she finishes her work. Sometimes children distract themselves by asking for help repeatedly. In order to prevent this, I would recommend having them save the questions for later, after she tries to complete the work by herself. After she completes the homework, don't forget to pat her on the back and to praise her generously for the hard work she has done, even if it's not perfect.

Case Study

I had an 8-year-old client, Armando, who was extremely hyperactive. Armando was put on medication to control his hyperactivity. The medication controlled his activity level for the most part, but he still had difficulty completing his tasks in school, and as a result, his grades continued to suffer.

Armando was lighthearted and funny and apparently enjoyed his role as the class clown. I consulted with his mom and talked to her about the basics of natural and logical consequences. Even without direct intervention by the teacher, his mom was able to help him control his behavior in class.

She told him that if he feels like he just has to have fun during class, that he could make up for what he missed in class during his study time at home. The more he missed in class, the longer his study time.

The mom and the teacher agreed on a plan, which they referred to as a long-term investment in maintaining everyone's sanity. The teacher sent home a short progress report about what my client missed during the class.

If Armando happened to "lose" the report, he received the maximum allowable study time for that day (he "lost" the progress report only once during the entire experiment). He also had to write a report for his mom about what he learned during the make-up session. Armando quickly learned that he was making more work for himself and responded readily to this logical consequence.

Combatting Argumentativeness

If a child is oppositional and argumentative, sometimes the best course of action is to turn away from the argument. You do not have to get sucked into a shouting match. Instead, you can give them choices and then respect their choices, even if you disagree with them. As always, remember to follow through with either rewards or consequences.

It's critical that you keep your cool, while remaining honest about your feelings. For example, if your teenage daughter refuses to do her homework, instead of arguing with her, you can talk to her in a calm and respectful manner.

If she tries to leave the house to go visit her friend down the street, you can casually ask her about her homework. "Did you get a chance to finish your homework?" If she says, "No, but I will once I get back," you can calmly tell her that she can go after she finishes her homework.

If she tries to argue with you, you can interrupt her matter-of-factly and firmly let her know, "You can either do your homework and then go to your friend's house, or if you don't feel like doing your homework yet, you can stay home. You can help me with the dinner, if you want."

She may stomp off and go to her room instead. After a while, she may get bored and try to watch the TV. Again, you can calmly respond, "You can watch the TV, go to your friend's or whatever you'd like after you finish your homework. Or if you don't feel like doing your homework yet, you can find something to do in your room."

Summary:

- Research indicates a combination of medication and parenting skills training is one of the most effective approaches in working with children with ADHD.
- Natural and logical consequences can be highly effective in working with children with ADHD or oppositional behaviors.
- Limit their choices to two in order to avoid overwhelming children with ADHD.
- Block out distractions to help them focus on their tasks.
- Don't argue with children; but firmly and calmly follow through with logical consequences.
- Keep your cool with an argumentative child.

Chapter 10

Children with Serious Conduct Problems

The following are possible signs of serious conduct problems:

- Physical Aggression
- Stealing
- Vandalism
- Lying or dishonesty
- Difficulty taking responsibility for their actions
- Blaming others for their involvement in illegal activities (such as breaking and entering, using or selling drugs, etc.)
- Gang affiliation or involvement
- Academic difficulties
- Behavioral problems in school
- Disregard for rules or authority
- Aggressive towards animals
- Destroys property or engages in arson
- Repeatedly runs away from home or tries to run away
- Frequently truant
- Threatens to harm others

- Is vengeful
- Sexually abuses younger children
- Exploits others for their benefit
- Has difficulty maintaining healthy friendships
- Displays narcissistic tendencies (is self-centered or has entitlement issues)

It's very difficult for parents to discipline children with major conduct problems. However, parents can still rely on natural and logical consequences to help them cope with some of the challenges. You can use these techniques on a child, but you can also confront him, especially if he has difficulty taking responsibility for his actions.

Children Involved in Illegal Activities

You can use a combination of logical consequences and confrontation on children who try to "con" others. Be matter-of-fact in your confrontations and keep your emotions in check. If you "lose it" emotionally, it gives them power to test your limits even further. It appears as if they derive some sort of pleasure or satisfaction from knowing that they have pushed your buttons.

If a child is involved in criminal activities, it's extremely important that you allow her to experience legal consequences. She needs to be responsible for her choices and deal with some of the realities in life. Some would refer to this as "tough love," and it is tough. But parents need to find the strength to carry it out for their child's benefit.

As children grow older, you want to prepare them for the real world. If you didn't love them, you wouldn't be invested in their future. You wouldn't take the time and the effort to teach them. Most importantly, you wouldn't have the strength to put your emotional needs aside for their benefit in the long run. You need to restrain yourself from verbally lashing out at them and let them learn from their choices.

If you rescue them, they learn that they can get away with their inappropriate behaviors or their illegal activities. They learn to rely on you to "let it go just one more time." You can actually sabotage your efforts to teach them to be accountable for their behaviors. Children need to learn that they are responsible for their choices and the ensuing consequences.

I recently interviewed a 20-year-old man, who was diagnosed with Conduct Disorder as a teenager. I asked him what he thought parents should learn about raising teenagers. He said that the most important thing for parents is to be consistent in carrying out consequences for their children.

After a while, he clarified that parents shouldn't scold their children but that they should teach them to be responsible. He also believed that teenagers should learn to take care of themselves as they get older and that they should work for what they want.

He talked about his 13-year-old stepbrother. His brother was recently caught smoking marijuana in school. He also had a couple of failing grades on his report card. However, he refused to go to the regular summer school. Out of desperation, the father and the stepmother decided to send him to a special summer camp where he could attend "summer school" while taking part in various recreational activities.

After the camp, his parents sent him to Hawaii to stay with his friend's family. While in Hawaii, he was caught stealing a T-shirt. The boy's excuse for stealing the shirt was that he "couldn't be bothered" with getting his wallet from the car.

Children with conduct problems often rationalize their behavior. They may have distorted "criminal thinking patterns" that allow them to engage in illegal or antisocial activities without much remorse. One of my friends refers to this as "flexible morality." A child who takes a twenty-dollar bill from the kitchen table might excuse his behavior by saying, "Well, they shouldn't have left it around. What do they expect people to do?"

Although it's excruciatingly difficult, sometimes it may be the best thing for you to allow your children to suffer the legal consequences for their actions. What you are doing is teaching them what's appropriate in our society.

If a child breaks the law at age 13 or 14, assuming it's not a murder or another serious crime, he may be sent to the juvenile detention center or other legal facilities. Having him sent to these places for minor crimes may be a far more loving thing to do than allowing him to grow up as an irresponsible adult. I would prefer that a child learn to be accountable for his actions rather than have him sent to a high security prison for a major crime committed in his adult life.

One may argue that children may learn about committing more serious crimes in such places. Although that is a possibility, they still learn there are legal consequences, even for a child. They can learn that the punishment can be harsher for an adult, even for the same crime.

I have a 23-year-old friend. Although he's currently success-ful in his professional career and a model citizen, he was very difficult as a teenager. In fact, he engaged in various illegal activi-ties and had more symptoms than necessary to be diagnosed with Conduct Disorder. However, immediately after he turned 18, he stopped engaging in these behaviors. I talked to his parents, and they said they had no idea how he turned out the way he did.

I asked my friend what he thought helped him to turn around after he turned 18. He looked at me and simply said, "Well, I knew that after I turned 18, I wouldn't be able to get away with all that stuff."

When he was 15 years old, he spent a day and a half at a juvenile detention center for helping his friend steal a car and run-ning away to California. He wasn't sure why he only had to spend a day at the detention center, but he learned from the experience that he didn't care to go back to the center. From that day on, he was careful about what he did. He still engaged in questionable behaviors, but they weren't as deviant as they were prior to his confinement in a lockup facility.

Cruelty towards Animals

Some children may be cruel towards animals. Additionally, they may engage in arson or act out sexually with younger children. With these children, parents should limit access to animals, lighters or matches, and younger children. As with any serious behavioral problems, close supervision is recommended to monitor the child's behavior. I also strongly recommend an in-patient treatment center for these children.

During the sessions, I often encourage younger children to engage in play therapy. If the child is cruel towards animals, I actually model for the child, using stuffed toys, how to be gentle and kind towards animals. I also teach her to be patient, loving and nurturing with the toys.

With very young children, I explain, "Even though you see animals or people hurt each other in cartoons, it's not okay to hurt animals or people in real life. Cartoons are not real. They're 'just for pretend.' You know, like when you draw a picture of a dog, it's not a real dog. It's just a picture. But, if you try to do what they do in cartoons, you can end up really hurting or killing others. And if the animal dies, it means you can't see the animal ever again, because it can't come back to life. And that'll be sad if you can't ever see your dog again."

Due to their limited cognitive or moral development, I try to avoid using abstract concepts. I stay away from trying to explain that hurting others is wrong. However, I may ask them, "Hey, does it hurt when someone hits you?" They usually agree with me and they also admit they get angry if someone hurts them or treats them in a mean way. Then, I continue, "You know, that's how others feel when you try to hurt them. Even dogs don't like to be hurt, just like you don't. So, it's not okay to hurt animals or people, but it's definitely okay to pet your dog or to give people good hugs."

Gang-Affiliation

If a child is involved in a gang or tries to join a gang, it's best to intervene as soon as possible. This is the case even if you suspect that he is in any way affiliated with a gang.

Children want to join gangs so they can feel like they belong to a group, or so they can feel a sense of power from having others fear them. Sometimes they want to join gangs because they are bored or because of negative peer pressure. I often work with children who are gang "wannabe's." They just act as if they belong to a gang so they can appear "cool" in front of their peers.

If your child is already involved in a gang and is caught doing illegal activities, it may be best for him to suffer the legal consequences. If the legal system is not involved, you can try to restrict his freedom at least to some degree.

By this time, a child may be beyond respecting his curfew. You can still restrict his freedom by not allowing him to borrow your car to go over to "a friend's house" on a Friday evening. After you hide the keys, you can tell him, "You can invite your friends over if you'd like, as long as they're okay by me" (you don't want him to invite friends who are involved in a gang).

You may want to keep up with the current trends in gang-related clothes, language, signs and even mannerisms. The local police department can help in educating you about these matters. Police officers from the special gang unit are also available for community outreach programs. Such programs can help alert you if a child is already in a gang or if he's affiliated with a gang. They can also give you guidelines or suggestions to follow in order to reduce the risk of your children becoming involved with a gang.

If it appears that your child is indeed in a gang, you can confront her matter-of-factly. If you are not sure, it may be best to ask her, rather than assume that she's involved in a gang. Many parents hesitate to ask their teenagers such questions because they believe they may not get a straightforward answer. Or, perhaps, they're afraid that they will. It's amazing how children can be open and honest with you, if you talk with them respectfully and matter-of-factly.

Although you can't watch over your teenager 24 hours a day, you can censor his video games, movies, books, music and clothes at home. I believe in freedom of speech, but not when it interferes with children's health, safety and well-being.

I believe I do my part in advocating for children's rights. However, children often do not have the experience or the wisdom that adults do, in filtering out materials that are bad for them. This is where you, as an adult, can step in and limit what they're exposed to, especially since it's a critical time for them.

They're more susceptible to being caught up in negative cultures or influences if they're primarily exposed to these things. The best way to counter this is to surround them with a positive environment.

As always, the best approach is the preventive approach. You should get your young children involved in activities or associations, such as volunteering in different community activities and participating in leadership groups. If they're too busy doing positive things, it gives them less time to focus their energy and time on negative things. This is another reason why I try to ask children to help me with things that I really don't need help with, just so I can distract them.

Physically Aggressive Children

If 7-year-old Tomeka is physically aggressive towards other children, her mother, Opal, can tell her that it's not okay to bite, hit, or kick others when she's angry. She can let Tomeka know it is okay to feel angry, but that it's not okay to hurt others.

Opal can also teach Tomeka to express her feelings with words, rather than through physical aggression. She can use a similar approach in letting Tomeka know that it is not okay to break or vandalize other people's property.

Case Study

Recently, I had a 5-year-old client, Maurice, who threatened to hit me during our final session. When I first started seeing Maurice, he was extremely aggressive towards the other children in the home. He was also physically aggressive toward his foster parents. His foster parents used the approaches outlined in this chapter. After several weeks, Maurice stopped being physically aggressive altogether, although he continued to threaten others during his infrequent tantrums.

I tried to prepare him about a month in advance for our last session, but when the last day came, he wasn't too happy about saying goodbye to me and regressed during the last session. Maurice was a little difficult, like he used to be when I first started seeing him. He acted as if he didn't hear me at times and he acted out during the session.

I tried to validate his feelings and I told him that I could tell he didn't want to say goodbye to me. Then, I asked him how he felt about our final session. At this point, he raised his voice and yelled, "Stop talking. You're giving me a headache!" I remained silent and allowed him to continue coloring his picture in silence.

After a while, I gently told him that we needed to talk about saying goodbye today because it would help us feel better if we talked about it. Well, I didn't get the response that I wanted. Instead, he shot me a menacing look and threatened, "If you don't stop talking, I'm gonna hit you!"

I automatically responded, "I don't think so," and continued to pretend that I was busy writing. Inside, I was saying, "Oh, God, please don't let him hit me. I don't know what I'd do if he hit me."

In ten years of working with children, not one has ever hit me, and I've worked with many, many children with serious behavioral problems. Maurice paused and looked at me, not knowing what to say. I looked back at him with a flat expression on my face, hoping desperately that he couldn't read my mind.

He said, "I really am gonna hit you! I mean it!" I calmly told him, "I know you wouldn't hit me." Then, I quickly changed the subject. I got up and opened the curtains. I pretended to be intently interested in what was outside. I looked around and asked, "Are there birds out there? I think they're singing!"

He got up right away and joined me at the window. He looked out, searching for the birds. I was relieved when he found some. He became excited and pointed towards them; and he said, "There they are!" And I praised him for having good eyes.

After reestablishing our rapport, I decided to write him a good-bye letter, in which *I* would talk about how I felt about our last session. I read the letter out loud as I was writing it. Using this approach, he was able to process his feelings about our termination.

If a child is physically aggressive at the time you try to intervene, you may have to restrain him (by holding him) or confine him to a safe environment, where he won't be able to hurt himself or others. But try to be careful while restraining him, especially if he has been physically or sexually abused in the past.

As you are restraining him, you can calmly let him know that this is not a punishment and that you are just trying to help him and everyone stay safe. It's important to let him know that the restraint or the confinement is only temporary, in order to allow him some time to calm down or to give him a break from others.

Most foster parents can rely on their training to restrain children appropriately. However, biological parents or other caregivers may need to take classes so that they can restrain their physically aggressive child safely and effectively.

If the child is extremely dangerous due to his size, strength or use of weapons, I strongly recommend having him assessed for an inpatient psychiatric treatment. Such settings can be used temporarily for crisis management or for emergencies. They can prescribe psychotropic medication to help control his mood or violent behaviors.

Stealing

With children who have problems with stealing, I usually use logical consequences. I also try to give them as much control as possible. In my experience, a combination of these two approaches, has proven to be very effective with these children, especially because they often have power and control issues.

Some children also have a need to relieve their anxiety by stealing. It almost appears as if they're addicted to stealing and that they're able to get some relief from their anxiety by giving into their need to steal.

If a kid has a problem with stealing, you may want to first remove his opportunity to steal. It's very tempting for him if he sees a twenty-dollar bill on the kitchen counter. A child may see it as an open invitation to steal. This may mean that you have to lock up your valuables. It can be inconvenient for you, as well as for other members of the family. However, until he learns to control his impulse to steal, this may be the best course of action for everyone.

Your ultimate goal is to have him monitor and discipline himself without your supervision or intervention.

You may want to tell the other kids to let you keep their money or valuables, and you can assure them by keeping a log of their "account." In using this approach, be careful not to shame the child with the stealing problem. Instead, you can explain to the other children that this is for everyone's benefit, without pointing any fingers. Encouraging them to keep their belongings and prized possessions in a safe place can also help them to be more responsible.

There should be a rule to discourage children from going into each other's rooms without permission. If a child has difficulty following these rules, you can have him "shadow" you around the home, so you can supervise him at all times.

When going to the store, you can also require him to be with you at all times. If this proves to be a problem for whatever reason, you can cut down his privilege of accompanying you to the store, until stealing becomes a less of a problem.

All these consequences are logical; they relate to the problem. They are not intended as a punishment; instead, they're a logical way of coping with this problem. It decreases a child's opportunity to steal. You can matter-of-factly let him know that he can earn your trust back *over time*, by consistently respecting other people's property.

Dishonesty

You can use a similar approach in working with a child who has a problem with dishonesty. For instance, with younger children, I may tell them I'm not sure if I can believe them when they tell me they would like another piece of candy. I explain that it's difficult for me to believe them because they keep on telling me things that aren't true.

Often, younger children try to tell me they were just kidding or that they were just trying to trick me. In this case, I tell them it's difficult for me to know when they're just trying to trick me. Then I let them know that since it's difficult to tell when they're telling me the truth or when they're just "joking around," I don't know if I can trust them when they say they want another piece of candy.

I smile and gently tell them that they need to earn my trust back. Also, I reassure them that they can do this over time and that I do want to trust them again. And, as always, when I know that they are telling the truth, I praise them and let them know I appreciate it when they tell me the truth. I also back that up with a pat on the shoulder.

Children with Narcissistic Characteristics

I work with many teenagers. Most of them display at least some narcissistic characteristics, which I believe is normal for their developmental stage. It's normal for teens to be self-focused and self-centered at least to some degree.

However, there are other teenagers who have a serious problem with narcissistic tendencies. They believe that the rules shouldn't apply to them or that people should make special concessions for them.

When I hear teenagers making such comments, I smile and tell them, "You know, I think you *are* very special. But I have news for you. The world does not revolve around you." I say this only when I've developed a sufficient rapport with them; otherwise, I may hurt their feelings.

I may continue, "We all have to stop at stop lights. We all have to pay taxes. Even special people like you. Of course, you can choose to go through the red light, and you can choose to not pay your taxes. But you can also choose to get a ticket and choose to go to jail."

It's been my experience that to make long lasting changes for these children, they have to learn to be sensitive and compassionate with others. When they're focusing on other people's needs or feelings, it's difficult for them to be self-focused and narcissistic.

Summary:

- It's very difficult to parent children with serious conduct problems. However, you can use natural and logical consequences to cope with some of the challenges.

- You can confront children or teenagers to help them take responsibility for their actions, especially if they try to rationalize their inappropriate behaviors.

- Allow children to experience the legal consequences when they break the law.

- It is critical that parents restrain themselves from rescuing their children.

- If a child is a danger to himself or others or if he is cruel towards animals, you should take precautions and limit his opportunities by providing increased supervision.

- Sometimes, a child may need to be hospitalized due to his dangerous behaviors.

- It is extremely important to develop empathy in these children.

- Be aware of the possible signs of gang affiliation or gang involvement.

- A multidisciplinary, preventative and community-based approach can be used in countering the effects of gangs in your neighborhoods and in your children's schools.

- Teach physically aggressive children to cope with their feelings by using logical consequences and by teaching them appropriate social skills.

- Decrease a child's physical aggression by validating her feelings and by teaching her to express her feelings appropriately.

- Distractions can be highly effective in redirecting younger, physically aggressive children.

- It may be necessary for you to restrain a child for his or others' safety.

- Stealing may be a child's attempt to gain a sense of control over his anxieties.

- Restructuring a child's environment can help to minimize his opportunity to steal from others.

- Confront children who are dishonest. You should also confront children who have problems with stealing and follow through with logical consequences.
- Developing empathy is critical in helping children with narcissistic tendencies.

Chapter 11

Sexually Abused Children

The following are potential indicators of sexually abused children. Please note that they do not have to display all of these symptoms. However, they often exhibit several of these symptoms at once. The presence of one or a few of these symptoms may not indicate that the child was abused. Please refer to the Appendix at the end of this book for a list of resources pertaining to sexually abused children.

- Has symptoms of a sexually transmitted disease
- Is pregnant
- Is knowledgeable about sexual subjects beyond his or her age
- Tries to sexually act out with other children or adults (e.g., exposes himself, tries to touch other children's private parts, talks about explicit sexual matters, etc.)
- Is very sensitive to touches that are not sexual in nature
- Acts or dresses provocatively
- Wears layers of clothing, even during the warm seasons
- Has nightmares or night terrors
- Tries to be the perfect child

- Displays a marked decrease in school performance
- Has problems with drugs or alcohol abuse
- Exhibits unusual behaviors
- Masturbates either privately or in public
- Is preoccupied with sex, private parts and other sexual matters
- Has enuresis (wets the bed/clothing) and/or encopresis (soils the bed/clothing)
- Exhibits self-abusive or self-mutilating behaviors (e.g., has superficial cuts on the wrist, scratches herself until she bleeds, etc.)
- Tries to run away from home repeatedly
- Engages in regressive behaviors (e.g., thumb sucking, baby talk, etc.)
- Is more needy and clingy than usual
- Shows a high level of anxiety, fears and nervousness
- Displays various psychosomatic illnesses (e.g., stomachache, headache, nausea, etc.)
- Isolates himself from other children, adults or activity
- Loses concentration or focus easily
- Is hyperactive
- Refuses to change clothes and has problems with hygiene
- Draws sexual pictures beyond his or her age and/or engages in sexualized play with toys or dolls
- Has a low self-esteem (e.g., makes negative comments about himself)
- Cries for no apparent reason
- Either overeats or frequently refuses to eat
- Makes suicidal statements or attempts
- Exhibits insomnia or oversleeps

How to Talk to Children When They
Disclose about Incest or Sexual Abuse

Children need to learn about the various safety rules regarding personal boundaries and private body parts. My youngest client was two and a half years old. She was sexually abused by a 12-year-old in her neighborhood. I believe children should be taught about these safety rules as soon as they're able to communicate and understand simple sentences. However, care should be taken in using developmentally appropriate words.

If a child exhibits many of the symptoms listed above, and if there are drastic changes in her behavior or mood, I highly recommend that she be assessed by a professional therapist for possible sexual abuse. Your need to know if something has happened to your child may have to wait until you can get your child in for a professional assessment. This is extremely important for your child's emotional welfare. Of course, you want professionals to intervene immediately if you know your child is pregnant or if she has a sexually transmitted disease!

Parents often take it upon themselves to assess for possible abuse. Sometimes, circumstances compel parents to ask their children about the abuse. Since this is the case, I'd like to make several recommendations in order to help you in the process. There are things you can say to comfort children who have been sexually abused. However, you can also unintentionally say something or respond in a way that can prove to be traumatic for your child.

It's best not to ask leading or specific questions, and you should allow the child to talk to you in a place where she feels safe. Again, if you are uncomfortable or afraid of how you might react to her disclosure, it's best to take her to a child therapist who specializes in sexual abuse.

If you decide to talk to her, you may want to begin with a general, non-threatening question. For example, you can say, "Susie, I've noticed that things have been a little different lately. You used to come home and talk to me about what happened at school. And you used to go out to play with the other kids. But for the last few days, you've been staying in your room most of the time. I've been kinda worried about you. Did something happen that you'd like to tell me about? If something is wrong you can tell me, no matter what."

It's possible and often very likely that she may not disclose about the sexual abuse or the incest. If this happens, you can respond, "It's okay, Susie. You don't have to talk about it right now. But I want you to know I love you and I care about you. There's nothing that's going to change how much I love you. I just want to take care of you and keep you safe."

If she does disclose that she was abused, the most important thing to remember is to remain calm. This is not to say that you have to be "a fake." However, it is very important that you stay calm during the initial disclosure. Again, you shouldn't ask her leading questions or pressure her to answer your questions (for your child's well-being, as well as for legal reasons).

If a child looks frightened and refuses to answer any more of your questions, you can tell her, "It's okay. I know it's scary to talk about what happened. I'm not going to make you talk about it right now if you don't want to. Maybe you can talk about it next time. I just want you to know that you didn't do anything wrong and that you're not in trouble for what happened. And I'm glad you told me what happened. You were very brave!"

It is extremely important that you don't show shock or extreme anger towards the perpetrator. Tell her that you are sorry she was abused. You can tell her that the perpetrator shouldn't have abused her and that the abuse wasn't her fault. It may be comforting for her to hear that you are glad that she told you what happened and that she was brave for telling you about the abuse.

You shouldn't yell that you're going to get the perpetrator and put him away for life. Instead, you can comfort your child by telling her that you will do whatever you can to get some help for the perpetrator, so that he (or she) won't abuse her or anybody else again.

Additionally, you need to let her know that no matter what happens, that you love her and that you will stand by her and protect her. It's very important that you let her know that you will take care of her and you will find help for her, as well as the family, to help everyone get through what happened.

Sometimes, children tell me that they want to kill the perpetrator or they wish the perpetrator were dead. In this case, I respond, "I can tell you're very angry. You just want him to go away and stay gone!" I refrain from telling them they shouldn't say that, and I try not to agree with them either; I merely validate their feelings.

If the abuse occurred long before the initial disclosure (whether it was a month or five years ago), you shouldn't ask her, "Why didn't you tell me what happened earlier?" She may feel as if the abuse were her fault for not telling someone sooner. Instead, you can gently and calmly ask her when the abuse occurred.

A younger child may have difficulty with the time concept and may refer to the abuse that happened two weeks ago as "a long time ago." If she discloses about the abuse in January, we can ask her, "Did he start touching you before Christmas or after Christmas?"

After she answers, you can continue, "How many times?" If she looks confused, we may have to ask her a leading question, "One time or more than once?"

It's very important that you remember to be matter-of-fact and to reassure her as you talk to her. You shouldn't overwhelm her with questions, and you should restrain yourself from nodding your head or otherwise encouraging her to agree with you.

Care should be taken with your tone of voice, your body language and your facial expressions. A defense lawyer may accuse you of leading her into making false allegations. You can reassure her by having a calm demeanor and letting her know it's okay to tell you what happened.

The child's feelings should be validated. If she appears to be scared in telling you who abused her, you can let her know that it's okay to be scared. However, you shouldn't tell her how she should feel. For instance, refrain from saying, "Don't be scared. You have nothing to be scared about." It would be somewhat abnormal for a child not to be scared in this situation.

And there are some instances in which children probably have a good reason to be scared. Perpetrators sometimes threaten to hurt them. Or the perpetrator may tell the child that she won't be able to see him any more if she tells anyone about their secret.

If she appears to be scared during the disclosure, you may want to say, "I can tell you're pretty scared right now. That's okay." As you pat her on the back gently, "You don't have to tell me who it is right now. But I'm going to do whatever I can to protect you from now on."

When a child's feelings are validated, she is more likely to talk openly about what happened. If she asks you what's going to happen now that she has told, you want to be as honest as possible. However, you don't need to give her every detail about what's going to happen.

Most likely, you won't know either, especially when you're dealing with the legal system. But, you don't have to let her think that you're "clueless" either. She needs to feel like you are in charge of things. You don't have to lie to her, but you can let her know that you're taking care of things.

Reporting Laws

Whether a child discloses past or current sexual abuse, adults are required by law to report the disclosure to a child protective agency in the state. When reporting, be as specific and as accurate as possible.

If you are not sure about something, such as the time frame in which the abuse occurred, then you need to let the worker know that you're not sure about when the abuse happened. Some of the questions may be difficult for you to answer emotionally. However, be as cooperative as possible, and try to answer all the questions.

Ask the worker if and when the agency will interview your family, including your child, about the allegation. In some cases, your child may be removed from your home, at least temporarily, for her safety. Although this may be difficult for you, you need to cooperate with the system for your child's safety.

Child protective agencies usually do not remove children from their home or their families without a very good reason. They understand that it's difficult for the family, as well as the children. Therefore, these agencies remove children when there is strong evidence to indicate that the child is in danger of physical or sexual abuse or neglect.

Ask the worker about the legal process and how you can help your child through the process. Make sure that you tell the worker that you do not want your child to be re-traumatized by repeated interviews.

Informing Your Child about the Interview

If the worker wants to interview your child, or if she plans to have your child interviewed by another worker, matter-of-factly inform your child about the interview, with the worker's permission. Sometimes, the worker may have a good (and legal) reason for not alerting children about the interview.

You can say, "Susie, some people are going to come over here tomorrow to talk about what happened. I just talked to them, and they sounded *real* nice. All you have to do is tell them what happened and tell them the truth. It'll be real quick. They're going to want to talk to you by yourself, but I'm going to be in the next room waiting for you. I'll be right there when you get done."

If You Decide to Divorce or Separate from Your Spouse

In case of incest, if you choose to separate or divorce from your spouse, it's very important to let your child know that you are not separating or divorcing her dad/mom because she told about the abuse. You should let her know that this is what you chose to do (and, in some cases, that her dad/mom agreed to do) for everyone's well-being.

Throughout the conversation, make sure that you use a child-centered approach in talking to her. If she's young, you want to use words that she can understand. You can let her know that you had to divorce or separate from her dad/mom so everyone can be safe.

If the court allows your spouse or partner to have supervised visitation rights, you should let your child know that she would still get to visit her dad or mom. But remember to tell her that it will be supervised and that she will be safe during the visits. You can explain to her that there'll be someone there to watch them both to make sure everything's okay.

At times, the court may grant your spouse or partner unsupervised visitations due to the lack of evidence to support the abuse (especially if it involves a custody battle). In this case, I strongly recommend individual therapy for the child, so that her therapist can teach her about children's rights to protect themselves, to tell bad secrets and to seek help from trusted adults. Her therapist can prepare her for the visits without "coaching" her to say to anyone that she was abused.

Incest vs. Sexual Abuse

If a child discloses about sexual abuse outside of the family, it can be less complicated in some instances. First of all, there's usually no separation or divorce related directly to the abuse. Additionally, it can be less complicated emotionally as well. Having a parent sexually abuse her could be more devastating than being sexually abused by someone outside the family. She may not be as emotionally invested in the relationship with an outsider.

If Your Child Tries to Sexually Act Out

If your child tries to sexually act out by trying to touch other children's private parts or by masturbating in public, talk to him about the rules regarding private body parts and about the three different kinds of touches. Teach him about the importance of telling secrets as well.

Children who are sexually abused often try to violate other's boundaries without violating them sexually. They may try to hug others or touch others without their permission. In this case, talk to your child about personal body space. As a rule of thumb, tell him to respect other people's boundaries by staying at least an arm's distance away from them. You can explain that everyone needs personal body space. However, remind him that he can ask others for a hug and wait for their permission before hugging them. Your child can learn that it's okay to touch others as long as it's not on their private body parts *and* as long as he has their permission.

This approach can be used with your child if he tries to or if you suspect that he is trying to sexually abuse other children. Remember to be matter-of-fact in your conversation and let him know what's okay and what's not okay when it comes to touching.

I used to make home visits to foster homes for several years. It wasn't unusual to see foster children sexually act out with each other. Often, these incidents are "consensual" between same-age peers. In other words, there was no "victim" or "perpetrator" by legal definition. When children sexually act out, they're acting out what they learned from their perpetrator.

Sometimes children who haven't been sexually abused may participate in sexually acting out due to curiosity. Some of them are more susceptible to negative peer pressure even though they know what they're about to do is inappropriate. These children may, in turn, act out what they learned with other children.

Children can sexually act out in their foster or adoptive homes, basic care facilities, as well as residential treatment centers. Although there is no guarantee adults can take preventive measures to reduce the risk of these children sexually acting out in these settings.

Case Study

In one of the foster homes, we had a "refresher" session after a new child, Darren, moved into the home. Darren was sexually abused by his stepfather and his uncle. After he settled into the new foster home, he tried to sexually act out with the other children in the home.

I had already talked about respecting others' boundaries with the other children several months prior to his arrival. However, Darren's foster parents and I decided to have another family session, to have a "refresher" about boundaries as well as other related topics. We talked about personal safety rights, private body parts and about the touching rules. Additionally, we stressed the importance of telling secrets, not to get the other children in trouble but to ensure everyone's safety.

Case Study

In another foster home, there were two children who were highly sexualized as a result of their past sexual abuse. They had sexually acted out with each other on more than one occasion over a four-month period. Because the children were old enough to read and write, they had to sign a contract in which they agreed to stop sexually acting out with each other. Their foster parents and their case manager also signed the contract. The children agreed to the rules, after the rules were explained to them in detail.

During their sessions, I elaborated on the contract and talked about specific examples of sexual acting out in order to cover any "loop holes" in the contract. I also made it clear to them that the rules were not limited to those examples but that they included other situations.

I had them state other examples in their own words, so that I could make sure they understood the contract. They also agreed to the consequences if they decide to sexually act out again in the future.

Sometimes, children try to sexually act out with adults. Usually, they were sexually abused by an adult, and so they try to replay their past abuse by trying to act it out with another adult. I believe this is an attempt to relieve their anxiety. Instead of waiting to see if the new person is going to abuse them as well, they take control over the situation and try to "initiate" the abuse.

Case Study

I had a 5-year-old client named Selena several years ago. She was sexually abused by her grand-uncle.

During one of our sessions, we worked on her boundary issues. She stood in front of a full-length mirror. I sat on the floor next to her so I could be at her eye level. In the mirror, I pointed to the areas where it's okay to touch people with their permission.

Suddenly, Selena slid the tank top off her shoulder and exposed her breast area. I was shocked and speechless. But, somehow, I managed to look calm.

I matter-of-factly reached over to her tank top and put it back on her shoulder. Then, I causally told her, "It's okay to look at your own private parts when you're by yourself. But it's not okay to show your private parts to other people."

"Your mommy can look at your private parts, but only when she's giving you a bath. And doctors and nurses can see your private parts to make sure you're not sick. I know your 'grandpa uncle' used to look at your private parts, but what he did was wrong. You don't have to show him or anybody else (except your mom and the doctors) your private parts again from now on, not for any reason."

"If you want good touches, you can ask me for a hug, and you can hold my hand." After the session, she wanted to hold my hand on our way to the waiting room. I told her mom about what Selena had learned in therapy that day, and that we were just practicing giving each other "good touches."

Case Study

Six-year-old Jeremy was sexually abused by both of his parents and was highly sexualized during the sessions. He engaged in sexualized play with the dolls repeatedly.

After a few months, it appeared as if he had worked through most of his issues. However, he said he wanted to brush my hair with the toy hairbrush. I told him that he could.

I was hoping that Jeremy had moved away from focusing on his past abuse and had gone into the "nurturing stage." Many of my clients start cooking or begin nurturing the dolls when they move beyond their past sexual abuse issues. I believe this is their way of nurturing themselves and protecting themselves.

However, my client started telling me how pretty I looked, as he was brushing my hair. Instantly, I felt uneasy, but I didn't want to assume things. He continued to brush my hair, telling me how pretty I was. Then, suddenly, I felt him pull on the collar of my shirt to look down my back.

Instead of jerking up like I wanted to, I remained calm and causally turned around to face him. I told him, "I don't like it when you do that. You can brush my hair, and you can make me look pretty. But it's not okay to look down my shirt, because it's my body. It's not okay to trick people like that."

My client wasn't trying to be nurturing towards me; he was trying to sexually act out with me. I told him, "From now on, you can brush the doll's hair, or you can brush your own hair. But you can't brush my hair until you learn to respect my boundaries" (we had already talked about what it means to "respect" other people's "boundaries").

Teaching Kids about Boundaries and Personal Safety Rules

As a general rule, you can use the following approach. Ask the child, "Do you know where your private parts are?" If he shakes his head or tells you "no," you can continue, "Private body parts are the parts of our body that are covered up by our bathing suit when we go swimming. Point to what's covered up when you go swimming. (Pause at this point.) How about what's covered up when girls go swimming?"

Then, ask him what he learned in therapy about private body parts. If he has difficulty answering, you can remind him, "No one's supposed to touch your private body parts, and you're not supposed to touch anyone else's private parts. Doctors and nurses can check our private body parts to make sure our private parts are okay." You may want to stop at this point and have your child repeat what you said. You can remind him about the rules again or clarify your points.

You can continue, "Other people aren't supposed to show their private parts to you, and you're not supposed to show your privates. But you can touch your own private body parts because it's your body. But, you have to do it behind closed doors, where there's no one else around."

"If someone tries to touch your private parts or if they try to get you to touch their private parts, you can say, 'No!' in a real loud voice, and then get away and tell a grown-up you trust about what happened. You can definitely tell me. I'll do whatever I can to help you and keep you safe."

Your child should know that he can tell you what happened even if the perpetrator is someone you know. "You can tell me what happened even if it's somebody Mommy knows really well. Even if it's a family member or someone else who was very nice to you."

"If you tell somebody else about what happened because Mommy isn't around, and if that person doesn't believe you, you can just go tell somebody else!" It's a good idea to point out several people in advance, such as, his teacher, his grandmother or an older sibling.

Research indicates that for many victims, it's the inappropriate response of the non-offending adult that proved to be more harmful than the actual abuse. A parent can actually traumatize the child further if she accuses him of causing the abuse or if she indicates that she doesn't believe him. Therefore, it's very important that you let your child know that you believe him. Also, it's extremely important that you communicate that he is not to be blamed for the abuse, even if he didn't tell someone about the abuse right away.

Talk to your child about "the touching rules" and about different kinds of touches (good touches, bad touches and secret touches). Goodnight kisses on the cheek, hugs from the side and holding hands are some examples of "good touches." Examples of bad touches include hitting, kicking and biting. Secret touches have to do with when an adult or (usually) an older child touches a younger child *anywhere on the body* and tells the child to keep it a secret.

The reason I said *anywhere on the body* is because the perpetrator often tries to "groom" the child by touching him in appropriate places first before working his/her way to the child's private parts. Explain to your child that touching should never be a secret when it comes to children. He should know that he can tell others about secret touching even if someone tries to touch his elbow, "because touching should never be a secret when it comes to your body!"

Sexual Abuse and Dishonesty

In working with children over the years, I've noticed a phenomenon with sexually abused children. This was also evident in working with adults who were sexually abused as children. Most of the sexually abused children were either threatened to keep quiet about the abuse, or they were bribed to lie about the abuse. Often, a single lie may be turned into multiple lies to cover up the underlying truth. Although not all sexually abused children grow up to be dishonest, I've noticed that many of these children assume *dishonesty* as a coping mechanism.

During the sessions, I matter-of-factly let them know that although they may have learned to lie from the perpetrator, that they don't have to lie any more. I let them know it's okay to talk about the abuse and that it's okay to tell the truth. I remind them they're safe now to tell the truth about the abuse and about everything else.

When I catch a child lying during the session, I casually tell her, "Tiffany, I know that your stepfather taught you to lie about what happened, and other people may have taught you to lie as well. But, you don't have to lie anymore. It's okay to tell the truth."

"I know you probably told your mom that you didn't steal her money so you wouldn't get into trouble. But she found out the truth anyway, and you ended up getting into double trouble for lying, as well as stealing. You might as well tell the truth and get it over with. Better yet, if you don't steal in the first place, you don't have to deal with any of this mess. I hate to see you get into trouble. I know it's no fun!"

Regarding False Allegations

Sometimes, children in foster care or residential treatment centers make false allegations of sexual abuse. False allegations may happen more frequently in these settings than in the general public. However, you don't have to panic, because you can take precautions to counter false allegations.

First of all, *document, document, document*! In most instances, a thorough and competent investigation will quickly determine these allegations as "unfounded." But you must keep accurate and detailed records of your child's behaviors if they can be construed as sexual in any way.

Seeking Professional Help

Whether a child is a victim of incest or sexual abuse, I strongly recommend professional help for the child and her family. Her family may be devastated and their lives disrupted due to the abuse. For instance, the victim's brother may blame his sister for making their dad move out of the house. Or, worse, he can blame himself for the abuse.

Case Study

I had a client who was sexually abused by her step dad. Tammy had a brother who was two years older. I took turns providing individual, sibling and family sessions. After a while, it became evident that Tammy's brother, James was blaming himself for his sister's abuse because he didn't stop the abuse when their dad made him watch the abuse.

During the sibling session, I told them that their dad should not have abused Tammy and that their dad should not have made James watch the abuse. "It wasn't you guys' fault. I don't think your dad's a bad person. But, what he did was wrong, and I hope he feels sorry for what he did. You guys aren't responsible for what happened, not even one percent!"

I explained to James that it wasn't his responsibility to protect his sister. "You guys were both little kids when this happened." James agreed that he was scared during the abuse. I told him that it was normal and that most kids *are* scared when they're being sexually abused or when they're made to watch the abuse.

James looked at me as if he were shocked. I said, "Yep. I know it's sad. But this happens to a lot of other kids too. And they understand how you guys feel." He appeared a little more relieved at this comment.

I continued, "If your dad didn't abuse Tammy in the first place, you wouldn't be feeling this way, like it was your responsibility to stop the abuse. There wouldn't have been anything to stop!" They both agreed with me.

"I hope your dad gets some help from a good therapist, so he won't sexually abuse anyone ever again! I hope he really feels sorry for what he did. And I hope one day he can admit what he did and apologize to you guys." They both agreed with me again.

I also recommend individual therapy for the non-offending parent in cases of incest. Incest is definitely traumatic for the child. However, it can also be devastating for the non-offending parent. In case of incest, the marital relationship is severely affected. To have a spouse or partner, whom you are intimately involved with, sexually abuse your child is devastating.

When choosing a therapist, whether it's a family therapist or an individual therapist, you should call around for a therapist who specializes in child sexual abuse. You may want to make sure that the therapist has at least a Master's degree in social work or in another counseling field.

Ideally, the therapist should have at least three or more years of experience working with sexually abused children and their families. One who's experienced in providing court depositions or testimonies regarding child sexual abuse and someone who's experienced in working with child custody cases can also be invaluable during the legal process.

During the sessions, the therapist should talk about private body parts and about personal safety rules. However, if a child tries to sexually act out in public, it's your responsibility to remind him about these rules. You can ask the therapist for her assistance in this situation.

Giving Kids Hope

Most sexually abused children are scared that they'll grow up to be an abuser as well. I let them know I understand how they feel, and I normalize their feelings. However, I also inform them that most abused kids grow up to be "helpers," such as doctors, nurses or teachers.

For most of them, this information comes as a surprise. I can tell from looking at their faces that this is the first time in which they feel hopeful about their future as adults. They realize they can become somebody who can actually help others, instead of hurt others like their perpetrators did to them.

Summary:

- Sexual abuse can have a devastating effect on a child's psychological and social well-being.

- It's important to learn to identify various warning signs that may indicate that a child has been sexually abused.

- When there are warning signs, it's best to seek professional help from a child therapist who specializes in working with sexually abused children, to assess for possible abuse and to work through the abuse issues.

- Everyone is required by law to report any suspected or known sexual abuse of a child.

- Use extreme caution when responding to children who disclose about sexual abuse or incest, but always let them know that the abuse wasn't their fault.

- It's best to refrain from asking leading questions or from forcing the child to disclose about the abuse.

- Younger children may have difficulty pinpointing when the abuse occurred due to their limited time concept.

- If you decide to divorce or separate from your spouse due to incest, your child should know that it isn't her fault.

- Individual or family therapy is recommended for the child and his siblings, as well as the non-offending parent, in case of divorce or separation.

- Children should be informed about upcoming interviews with child protective workers matter-of-factly, but they should not be coached in what to say during the interview.

- Different issues are associated with incest as opposed to sexual abuse by a non-family member.

- Children need to be educated about appropriate boundaries and personal safety rules as early as possible.

- There are measures that can be taken to prevent or stop children from sexually acting out.

- There are actions that can be taken to counter false allegations of child sexual abuse.

- Sexually abused children can be trained by the perpetrator to be dishonest; however, they can be retrained and re-socialized so they know they don't have to lie anymore.

- Most sexually abused children do not grow up to be perpetrators; instead, many of them grow up to be in the helping profession.

Chapter 12

Physically Abused Children

If you're a foster parent or an adoptive parent, you're probably aware if your child has a history of physical abuse. However, if you're a stepparent or another guardian who doesn't have a complete history of your child's background, the following list can serve as a guideline to determine if you should have your child assessed and treated for past physical abuse. Please refer to the Appendix for a list of resources related to physically abused children.

- Physical aggression
- Nightmares
- Enuresis and/or encopresis
- Self-abusive behaviors (e.g., head-banging)
- Difficulty making or keeping friends
- Academic or behavioral problems in school
- Scars or old burn marks
- Violation of others' boundaries (either physical or sexual)
- History of running away

- Symptoms of brain damage (e.g., seizures, difficulty walking, etc.)

- Overeating or loss of appetite

- Insomnia

- Symptoms of neglect

- Extreme isolation or shyness

- Verbally aggressive or threatening

- Tries to be the "perfect child"

- Attempts to emotionally "rescue" others in the family

- Steals and/or lies frequently

There are many similarities between sexually abused and physically abused children. The main difference, however, usually has to do with the child's "sexualized" behaviors.

Whereas a sexually abused child may masturbate in public, the physically abused child may be less likely to exhibit such behaviors. However, the latter may be aggressive, or he may misinterpret sudden movements and back away if someone were to raise a hand quickly, even if done in a non-threatening manner.

Many people believe that sexually abused children grow up to be sexual perpetrators. However, research indicates a stronger relationship between physically abused children and sexual perpetration later in adulthood. This supports the idea that rape is not merely a sexual act but an act of violence.

When Children Blame
Themselves for the Abuse

In processing about a child's physical abuse, I try to be very careful in validating his feelings no matter how he responds to the abuse. Sometimes, children blame themselves for the abuse. Naturally, I do not agree with them, but I validate their feelings and then try to normalize their feelings of guilt. However, I always explain to them that the abuse wasn't their fault.

A child may argue that his dad hit him because he had talked back or cursed when he wasn't supposed to. I may agree with him that it's not okay to curse at his parents. But I also point out that it's not okay for his dad to abuse him for that reason or any other reason. I tell my client that it's better for parents to give their child a time-out or some other consequence.

Post-traumatic Stress Disorder in Physically Abused Children

Case Study

I worked with two siblings who were removed from their home due to physical abuse and severe neglect. They were abandoned by their mother, and physically abused by their father. During the sibling session, the two boys would use every opportunity they had in talking about their past abuse.

They had assured me that their dad nor anyone else ever sexually abused them. Additionally, they didn't display any of the symptoms specific to sexually abused children. But they both had a diagnosis of Post-traumatic Stress Disorder (PTSD) from the physical abuse. They had nightmares, they were anxious, they both had enuresis and they focused on their past abuse repeatedly. So, I allowed them to talk about their abuse session after session.

The older sibling, Jesse, indicated that he hated his father. I validated his feelings and told him that he could hate his father and that he could be mad at him as long as he wanted to, until he stops being mad at his dad one day.

The younger sibling, Tom pointed out that he didn't hate his dad but that he didn't want to go back home to live with his dad either. I told him that it was okay to feel differently from his older brother. I validated his feelings as well and assured him that he would not have to move back home since both parental rights had been terminated.

Tom said he might visit their parents once he turns 18, since he'll be able to protect himself. I agreed with him and told him that he could visit them as an adult. I also told him that if he changes his mind about visiting them, that it was okay too.

I leaned over and told the two boys, "And while you guys are growing up, I hope your parents get some help, so they won't hurt anybody ever again." They both agreed with me.

As the sessions progressed, they talked less and less about their abuse and focused more on their current problems, such as school problems. Gradually, their symptoms improved; they stopped having nightmares and they stopped wetting the bed.

Getting Help for the Physically Abused Child

If you suspect that a child has been physically abused, I strongly recommend that the child be assessed by a therapist or a psychologist who specializes in working with physically abused children. As with sexual abuse, even if you *suspect* physical abuse, you are required by law to report it to a child protective agency.

If it is determined that he was indeed physically abused, I recommend individual, sibling and/or family therapy. To facilitate the process, however, I recommend that you work very closely with your child's therapist. Additionally, you can use similar suggestions about seeking help for the sexually abused child.

The Effects of Witnessing a Parent's Abuse

Many years ago I worked with battered women, and most of their children also suffered physical abuse from their fathers or their father figures. Additionally, they were often more traumatized from witnessing their mother's abuse than by their own physical abuse.

Case Study

Ten-year-old Mario was severely physically abused by his father. During the sessions, he played out witnessing his mother being beaten repeatedly by his dad. Mario did not use the dollhouse or the dolls, but instead he used dinosaurs to represent his family. Since it was apparent that this was his priority in therapy, we worked on his issues surrounding his mother's abuse first. We then worked on Mario's physical abuse issues.

I explained that his father should not have hurt his mother, and that he definitely should not have hurt her in front of him. I said, "Children shouldn't be made to watch things like that. I don't think your dad was bad, but he does have some serious problems with his anger. I hope he gets some help, so he can learn to handle his anger the right way. I hope he feels sorry for hurting you and your mom, and I hope that one day he'll apologize to you and your mom for what he did."

I also validated his feelings about witnessing his mom's abuse. He told me that he felt scared, sad and mad "all at the same time." I normalized his feelings and told him, "You know, almost all the other kids I work with tell me the same thing. They feel mad and sad, and even scared, when they see their mom or their sisters or brothers getting hurt by their dads. Sometimes, kids feel just sad or just mad, and that's okay too."

Privately, I shared these things with Mario's mother. Then, we had a family session in which I encouraged Mario to talk about his feelings about witnessing his mom's abuse. At times, I would speak for him if he had problems or if he was hesitant to speak for himself. I had his permission to do so prior to the family session. Additionally, I had asked Mario's mother prior to the family session to validate her son's feelings and to share her feelings about what happened.

Eventually, I asked the mother to let Mario know that she will do her best to take care of herself, as well as protect him from now on. I also asked his mother to refrain from talking "bad" about Mario's dad but to acknowledge that what he did was wrong.

I explained to her, "If you tell Mario that you hope his dad gets better and that you hope he doesn't hurt anyone else again, Mario may feel more secure or more at peace. But, if you were to yell that you hope his dad goes to jail or something like that, Mario may get scared or anxious that his dad might go to jail."

"I'm not trying to discourage you from filing charges against Mario's dad. I think you should do whatever's best for you and Mario, but Mario doesn't have to know the details. And he certainly shouldn't have to feel like he has to choose sides, or feel like it's his responsibility to put his dad in jail."

Summary:

- The primary difference between a sexually abused and physically abused child has to do with sexualized behaviors.
- Witnessing a parent's abuse can be more traumatic for the child than his own physical abuse.
- Children often blame themselves for the physical abuse; it's important that you communicate that the abuse wasn't their fault.
- Individual and family therapy are recommended for the child, as well as the non-abusive parent.
- Physically abused children may suffer from PTSD, just as sexually abused children suffer from their abuse.

Chapter 13

Children with Depression

The following symptoms may be an indication that your child is depressed:

- Frequent crying
- Overeating or loss of appetite
- Insomnia
- Decrease in academic performance
- Easily irritable
- Hygiene problems
- Isolation from friends
- Makes suicidal statements and/or attempts
- Slow speech or physical movement
- Makes degrading remarks about himself repeatedly
- Lack of energy or motivation in completing everyday tasks
- Hopelessness
- Poor concentration
- Hyperactivity

It should be noted that children who are grieving due to a family member's death might show some of these symptoms as well. Additionally, children may have some of these indicators if a parent is severely ill or in the process of dying.

Depression in children happens much more frequently than what is assumed by the general public. In fact, children as young as eight or nine years old have committed suicide as a result of their depression. Often, the adults in their lives are too depressed to recognize that their child is depressed as well.

Sometimes, parents may not be aware that their child is depressed if he appears to be hyperactive. They may think that their child has ADHD instead of depression. Or they may assume that their child is being difficult or oppositional.

Case Study

About two years ago, I had two sisters, Lydia and Kate, and their brother Jack in a sibling group. Normally, the oldest sibling, Kate, tried to be the "good girl" and was a positive role model for her two siblings. Although this was unhealthy in some respects (because it limited her ability to behave as a child), I usually allowed Kate to take on this role during the earlier sessions in order to build up her strength and confidence. I wanted to prepare her to work on more serious issues.

However, both of the biological parents' rights were about to be terminated. Their foster mom informed them of this news a few days before our next scheduled session. During our next session, Kate tested limits all over the place and was very argumentative. At one point, she broke down and cried because her sister would not let her use the crayons.

I calmly walked over to Kate and put my hand on her shoulder. Then, I gently told her that I could tell something was wrong and that I had a feeling that she was feeling "really, really sad." I pointed out that she wasn't behaving like she usually does, and I once again told her that I had a feeling that she was feeling really sad.

She started crying even more and yelled out, "It's because they won't let me see my dad or mom anymore!" I validated her feelings and said, "No wonder. I can tell you're sad and probably mad too. I know you want to see your mom and dad because you love them and miss them." She agreed with me that she had these feelings and that she wanted to see her parents. I asked Lydia and Jack how they felt about the news. They both agreed with their sister.

Later in the session, I asked them if they knew why they wouldn't be able to see their parents again, at least not until they each turned 18 years old. All of them said that it was because their dad did mean things to Kate (their father had sexually abused her). I asked them if they knew why they couldn't see their mom. They all said it was because she couldn't take care of them.

I agreed with them. I told them, "I don't think your parents are bad, but they do have some problems. Your parents knew they couldn't take care of you guys right now. They knew they couldn't make sure you guys stayed safe all the time. That's why they decided to let other people take care of you. This doesn't mean your parents don't love you, they just want to make sure somebody takes good care of you guys."

"But the good thing is you can all visit your parents once you turn 18." The children were happy about this, and we talked about what they would like to do when they grow up.

Interestingly, the oldest sibling said that she did not want to move back home with her parents but that she wanted to visit them "every once in awhile."

Summary:

- A child's depression can be masked by hyperactivity or by other behavioral problems.
- Very young children can suffer from depression as well.
- Children can become depressed for various reasons, ranging from the death of a family member to their parents' divorce.
- Parents should learn to identify warning signs for suicidal ideas or behaviors.

- Professional intervention is highly recommended if a child exhibits many of the symptoms for depression; a child may need in-patient psychiatric treatment in case of severe depression.

Chapter 14

Children of Divorce

If you and your spouse decide to get a divorce, you may need to explain to your child that you or your spouse will be moving out of the house and explain to him that it's because the two of you can't get along anymore. It's very important that you point out that he is not responsible for the separation in any way.

It's very comforting for a child to hear that his parents will not be "divorcing" him, that they'll still be his parents no matter what and that they still love him very much. You should let him know that his mom/dad will be visiting him, even though he'll be living with you. A note of advice: Please maintain a civilized relationship with your ex-spouse for your child's sake.

However, in case of incest, this may not be possible, especially if the court terminates the visitation rights. You may also want to rephrase how you talk to your children about the separation or the divorce. You should let him know that the separation is not his fault in any way. In case of incest, sexual abuse of another child, physical abuse or spousal abuse, you can tell him that the separation is necessary so that everyone in the family can stay safe.

Suggestions for Separated
or Divorced Parents

- Do not use your child as a messenger between you and your ex-spouse.

- Do not fight or argue with the other parent in your child's presence.

- If the other parent fails to show up for a visitation or changes his/her plans, do not criticize or accuse him/her of not loving your child.

- Do not make excuses about the missed visitations, but do validate your child's feelings of disappointment, anger, sadness or frustration.

- If the other parent misses the visitations often, talk to him/her about your child's reactions if your child's reactions are negative.

- Do not accuse your ex-spouse of any wrongdoing in front of your child.

- Try to use the problem-solving approach in working on any disagreements with your ex-spouse, rather than turning your conversation into an argument.

- Do not ask your child to report on the other parent or the other parent's new family.

- If your child's behavior is severely affected by the inconsistent visitations, you may need to take legal action for your child's welfare. Children can go through emotional turmoil, develop low self-esteem and act out due to the inconsistent visitations.

- With your ex-spouse, try to work out a similar schedule or similar rules for your child. If one parent has much more lenient rules than the other, the latter may be viewed as the strict or the "mean" parent.

- Try not to get rid of your guilt about the divorce or separation by buying your child material things or by being overly lenient with your child when it comes to consequences.

• Both parents should give the child plenty of love and affection, as well as positive touches.

• Let your child know that both you and your ex-spouse love him and care about him very much.

• If your child tries to "split" you and your ex-spouse (that is, work the two of you against each other in order to get his way), use your best judgement in carrying out consequences. Let your child know that you and your ex-spouse will talk about any discrepancies. In this way your child will know that there's a "working relationship" between the two of you when parenting is involved.

• Individual therapy is recommended for both parents in order to work through issues concerning the separation or divorce. If there is any hostility you haven't worked through, your child will probably pick up on it during your interaction with your ex-spouse.

• Children are very sensitive to their parents' feelings toward each other.

• If you have difficulty working through your feelings about your ex-spouse, remember your child's needs and remember to keep the interactions between you and your ex-spouse civilized.

• Try to coordinate and keep the visitation schedules consistent.

Example

I have a friend who got divorced a couple of years ago. He was married for 13 years to his high school sweetheart. He explained to me that they just grew apart over the years and that nothing dramatic led to their divorce.

However, a few months before the divorce, both he and his wife went through a stage where they hated each other. When I asked him what happened, he said, "I guess we just needed to create some conflict to distance ourselves from each other.

Currently, they maintain a good, civilized relationship with each other, partly because they still like each other, but mostly because of their two daughters.

Before the divorce was finalized, my friend and his wife sat down to negotiate the details of the new family situation. They told their lawyers to stay put and informed them that they would conduct the negotiations on their own. Their lawyers' job was limited to transcribing their compromises onto paper.

Initially, my friend and his wife agreed on a joint custody, where one would have the children for one week, and the other parent would have them the following week. However, they left it up to their daughters to make exceptions, just in case they wanted to go over to a friend's house or participate in a church activity. Their daughters were 9 and 11 years old, and my friend and his wife thought their girls should have a say-so in their lives.

Everything worked out okay, except the switching back and forth part. It was too much for my friend, his ex-wife, as well as the girls. They had to adjust, emotionally and otherwise, to the constant movement of the girls from one house to the other. So, the whole family agreed on switching the children's visits to every two weeks. And now everything's working out for the best, considering the circumstances.

My friend and his ex-wife keep each other informed about the major happenings in their girls' lives through frequent phone calls and e-mails. They also try to have consistent rules between the two households, so their daughters can feel secure about what's expected of them.

Best of all, my friend and his ex-wife live only a few streets down from each other. This was not a mere coincidence. They *intentionally* chose to live close to each other for their children's sake. They didn't think it was fair to make the girls fly across four states just to visit their parents.

Seeking Professional Help

When parents divorce or separate, I recommend individual or family therapy for the entire family. Family therapy can be provided for the custodial parent and/or for the non-custodial parent. The children should attend the sessions in either case. In some instances, I also recommend sibling therapy. During the sibling sessions, children may be more open in talking about their feelings because someone else understands exactly how they feel.

Children need a safe environment to process their parents' divorce or separation. The therapeutic process does not have to be long, but it can be an opportunity to talk about their feelings and to work out some new rules so that they can have some consistency in their lives.

Suggestions for the Partners of Non-custodial Parents

The following are some suggestions for partners of non-custodial parents during the visitations:

- Keep a civilized relationship with your partner's ex-spouse.

- Do not talk negatively about the child's custodial parent in front of the child.

- Have an open communication and clear understanding with the non-custodial parent about parenting issues.

- Make sure the child understands that both you and the non-custodial parent head the household and that the two of you determine and carry out the rules of the household. This includes rewards and privileges.

- Have the same rewards or consequences for both your biological child and your partner's child. Otherwise, it could be damaging for the latter's self-esteem. Favoritism can also contribute to the acting-out behaviors of the child, and may make your role as a caretaker even more difficult.

- Do not try to force the child to accept you as an authority figure. Let the child take her time to get used to the idea and your new role in her life.

- In carrying out rewards or consequences, it may be best to carry these out in front of the child's biological parent. This is especially important in the beginning of your relationship with the child. It can help you to transition your role as an authority figure to a "parent figure" due to the support from the biological parent.

Blended Families

Since about 50% of marriages end in divorce these days, there are many blended families just as there are many single-parent families. The children in "blended families" may have a new mom or dad, and they may have to learn to live with their new siblings, whether or not their stepparent has custody of his or her children.

With blended families, as with biological and foster families, both parents should take turns following through with logical consequences. Parents should carry out logical consequences for both their biological and stepchildren and not postpone the consequence until the arrival of the biological parent. They should also take turns passing out rewards or praises with all the children in the family.

Rules should be consistent among all the children, although they should be age-appropriate. It is especially important to keep open communications between the two families, especially when they get together for the first time. Although it's difficult, remember to initiate communication with your children and not wait for them to come to you first.

It is especially important in blended families to have family meetings and to play together. These activities are crucial in maintaining a bond with all the children in your family. One-to-one interactions with your stepchildren are also important, just as it is with your biological children.

Remember that the more stimulating the activity, the more effective it is in helping your family bond with each other. As in any family, you may want to talk to your spouse and agree (or at least, compromise) on parenting issues before talking to your children. If you fight or argue with your spouse in front of them, it can cause further "splitting" in the new family unit.

Chapter 15

When There is a Death in the Family

If a child is depressed due to a family member's terminal illness, try to prepare the child in advance. If someone in your family is in the process of dying, use a local hospice to help your family through the grieving process.

Hospice programs have doctors, nurses and social workers; they will educate and comfort your family. They can also help you talk to your children about death and dying, and they can provide you with opportunities for family members to have closure with the dying member.

Again, I recommend individual and family therapy in order to help your family through the dying process, whether the death of your loved one is sudden or prolonged. Because very young children have difficulty understanding the concept of death, it may be best to find a play therapist who can explain death and dying to your child at his or her level of understanding. If a family member dies suddenly, whether through an illness or by accident, they may think that the deceased person abandoned them. They take it personally and often think that they did something wrong to make the person leave them.

Since they don't understand the concept of death, they need someone to explain to them what death means. It is not a good idea to tell the child that the deceased person is asleep, or if you believe in heaven, that the deceased person won't wake up for a very long time. This may actually frighten the child, and he may refuse to go to sleep because he is scared that he may not wake up either. The child may also be afraid that the other family members won't wake up if they fall asleep. This can cause a high degree of anxiety about going to sleep and may cause additional problems, such as insomnia.

It is best to be honest with a young child, although you don't have to go into detail about death. If you believe in life after death, such as in heaven, you may want to explain to the child that when someone dies, it means that he and the rest of us will not be able to see the deceased person until we die a long time from now. You can point out matter-of-factly that most people live a very, very long time in order to lessen his anxiety.

Case Study

I had a 3-year-old client, Tina, whose older brother had died from an accident. In therapy, she told me that she was very angry with her brother, David, for not coming back home. In fact, she told me that she did not want to talk about her older brother. I validated her feelings and told her that other kids would feel the same way if the same thing happened to them.

I asked her if she knew what had happened to David. She told me that her brother had been in a car accident and that he had died from it. I asked her if she knew what it meant to die. Her mother had explained to her that David had gone to sleep for a very long time.

I told Tina that I knew she felt sad and mad about her brother not coming back home. However, I also explained to her that David did not die on purpose and that it was an accident. I said, "It's kind of like when you fall down and hurt your knees on accident. You don't try to fall down on purpose, but you do. Your brother didn't mean to get into a car accident, but he did."

I told her, "People won't be able to see him anymore, until they get really, really old. When they get really old, they die too and go to Heaven. Then, they'll be able to see him again in Heaven."

Because Tina did not have the concept of time yet, I separated my hands about six inches apart and explained, "Your brother lived this much." Then, I spread my arms apart as far as I could and said, "But, you see, most people live this much. I'll probably live this much too, and I bet you're going to live this much. Even your sister! Most people live for a long, long time until they get really, really old."

To check if she understood my message, I asked her to show me how long she thought her mother would live. Tina scrunched up her face and stretched her arms as wide as she could, and she emphasized it by stretching her legs as far apart as she could. She indicated that her mom would live a "long, long, long time."

I applauded and agreed with her. I explained that her brother loved her very much when he died and that he still loves her in Heaven. I told her that if she misses David, she could tell her mom and ask her for a hug. I assured her that this would help her feel better in the long run. I also told her that she could talk to her older sister and me, as well.

A few sessions before our termination, I had a family session with my client, her sister and both of her parents. I asked my client and her sister to write a goodbye letter to their deceased sibling. Tina and her sister were too young to write the letters by themselves, but they pretended and carefully made scribbles as if they were writing the letters.

I asked them to read the letter out loud, and I asked their parents to write down what they said. Both Tina and her sister acted as if they were really reading the letter, and their parents wrote what they said without interrupting them.

I had wanted them to write a goodbye letter to bring closure within the session. However, my client came up with a great idea. She wanted to put the letter in an envelope and take the letter to her brother's grave.

A few sessions later Tina's mother informed me that her kids read the letter out loud at David's gravesite. The parents also helped them bury the letter on top of the grave.

By the termination session, Tina no longer exhibited symptoms of depression. She wasn't physically aggressive toward her sister or towards the other children at daycare. She did not have as many tantrums or nightmares, and she stopped banging her head all together (during her tantrums, Tina used to bite others and bang her head against the wall).

With older children, it is equally important to have closure with the deceased person. Obviously, the same approach would not be used with an older child. However, writing a goodbye letter can be effective with children of any age in achieving closure, whether a family member has died or whether there's a separation due to divorce, etc.

As always, when there's a pressing issue such as a death in the family, individual and family therapy is recommended. Naturally, having a family member die can be traumatic for the family, especially for younger children. The death can be even more devastating for them if adults remain silent about it, because children may blame themselves for the death, or they may misunderstand what death means.

Often, my clients complain that it makes them feel worse to talk about sad things during the session. I know this can be true for adults as well. However, in the long run, being able to talk about our feelings somehow diminishes or lessens the painful feelings surrounding the traumatic event.

You can explain to your child that you understand it hurts to talk about sad things. However, you can assure her that although it may hurt while she is talking about the sad things, that she will feel better in the long run because she was able to get her feelings out.

You can say, "It's kind of like how it's easier to lift something heavy when you have somebody helping you. When you have somebody that you can share your feelings with, it's a lot easier to handle your feelings. It's as if the other person takes some of the pain away."

When there's a long period between the onset of the illness and the moment of death, there's an opportunity for the dying person to have closure with her family. If she's able to communicate, she can have a closure "session" or a meeting with her family.

Again, I highly recommend utilizing a hospice to facilitate this process. If the person or the person's family is religious, I also recommend asking a minister, priest or rabbi to participate in this meeting. This can be especially healing for the family members, as well as the dying person.

As in the previous example, children need someone to explain to them what's happening. A child's parent or another adult can talk to him about death, and explain that it's not his fault. If possible, the dying person should talk to the child.

However, I do not recommend this if the person is severely disfigured. The experience might traumatize the child. Young children may experience nightmares and engage in other behaviors, such as thumb sucking, bed-wetting, etc. from the experience.

Summary:

- If a child is depressed due to a family member's terminal illness, you can prepare the child in advance.

- Hospice programs can help educate and comfort your child and your family.

- Individual and family therapy are recommended to help the surviving members cope with the death of a loved one.

- Young children have difficulty with the concept of death and may need a child therapist to help them understand and process their feelings about the death.

- Family therapy can be a very effective way to achieve closure between the dying person and her family.

- It may be inappropriate for young children to visit the dying person or to attend the funeral, especially if the dying or the deceased person is disfigured.

Chapter 16

Bed-wetting

Your child may have problems with enuresis (bed-wetting or urinating in his clothes) or encopresis (soiling the bed or his clothes) for various reasons. Sometimes, it's due to a traumatic event. However, a moderately stressful situation can cause him to regress as well (such as, starting a new school year).

Often, enuresis and encopresis are accompanied by other regressive behaviors. These include thumb sucking, being clingy or needy and engaging in baby talk.

If a child is above four years old and has symptoms of encopresis, you should first consult a pediatrician to rule out any physiological basis for these symptoms. You should also check with the pediatrician if your child is past the age of five and has symptoms of enuresis. If the doctor determines that there's no physiological reason to explain these symptoms, individual and family therapy may be warranted.

As previously stated a child could have these symptoms if there's a separation or divorce, if he's been sexually or physically abused, etc. Starting a new school year or moving away to another city can set off "an accident." Often, these symptoms are temporary and will pass over time. Sometimes, however, these symptoms can last for a number of years.

Case Study

I worked with 8-year-old Paul and 9-year-old Kevin who had problems with enuresis for almost three years prior to our initial session. They were removed from their biological home due to physical abuse and severe neglect. With Paul, the symptoms were alleviated by the use of medication. However, Kevin continued to have accidents a few times a week even with the medication.

Kevin's symptoms worsened with the news that they would be moving away from their foster home to get adopted by a family from a different state. I asked the foster parents to respond to his accidents calmly. And, because he was old enough, I recommended that they allow Kevin to wash his own bedding and clothes.

I also cautioned them against lecturing him or embarrassing him about having the accidents in front of the other children. I asked them not to punish him for having the accidents and recommended that they limit his fluid intake two hours before his bedtime. Lastly, I suggested that Kevin be reevaluated for possible increase in his medication.

During individual therapy, we processed how Kevin felt about having enuresis. He indicated that he didn't like it and that he was embarrassed by it. I validated his feelings and explained to him that many children have this problem for various reasons.

He pointed out that his brother Paul didn't have any more accidents and asked me why he continued to have this problem. I matter-of-factly told him that different kids respond differently to the same medication or to the same situation.

I asked him what he thought was causing the problem. At first, he told me he didn't know. However, I said, "Why don't you use your imagination and come up with something good?" He quickly came up with a possible reason. "Maybe it's because of the adoption."

I nodded in agreement and asked, "How do you think it's related to the adoption?" He responded, "Well, I don't know." I encouraged him to think about the possibilities and asked, "Well, what do you worry about these days?" Again, he said, "The adoption."

I continued, "What are you worried about with the adoption?" After hesitating, he answered, "Well, I don't want to get adopted. What if they beat us up or something?" I restated what he said, "So, you're worried that your adoptive parents might abuse you guys?"

He agreed with me. I validated his concerns and continued, "And you think you have accidents because you're worried about how they'll treat you once you get adopted." He nodded his head.

I explained to him, "A lot of kids have accidents when they're worried about something or when they feel like they can't do anything about what's worrying them. But after they talk about these things and get it all out, they stop having the accidents for some reason. I think it's because they get to talk about their feelings, and they learn they can do something about whatever's worrying them.

"Like, did you know that CPS takes a long time to investigate people who want to adopt kids? Yep. They take a long, long time to try to make sure they're nice and safe. Oh, yeah, and they have to want kids really bad. And they have to be good with kids. CPS doesn't let people adopt kids if they know the people have a history of abusing kids."

Kevin looked a little more relieved, and we were able to process his feelings about the adoption and how he felt like a traitor for wanting to get adopted. He felt as if he were betraying his biological family by getting adopted. And he also felt sad about leaving his foster family.

We worked through these issues, and his accidents became less frequent. Several weeks later, my clients were adopted by a very "experienced family" outside the state. Shortly after the adoption, the ex-foster dad informed me that the boys seemed excited about their new family and that neither of them displayed any symptoms of enuresis, even without the medication.

With both enuresis and encopresis, the effects can be devastating for the child's self-esteem. He may isolate himself because he doesn't want to be embarrassed by the smell around his peers. More often, his peers could reject him because of the smell and because they don't want to be associated with a "baby."

Case Study

I had a 6-year-old client, Jamal, who had a problem with encopresis. During the initial session, I asked his dad if Jamal was ever referred to a pediatrician for this problem. I wanted to make sure there was no physiological basis for his symptoms. His dad indicated that he wasn't able to take his son to a pediatrician due to his financial difficulties. I referred the dad to a local non-profit organization to help him with the financial situation.

A couple of months passed, and Jamal's symptoms did not improve, although there was notable improvement in his social skills. During our individual session, Jamal told me that the other kids wouldn't play with him and that they called him names because of the "accidents" at school. We talked about using assertive communication to stand up for himself when other kids called him names. However, this didn't solve the root cause of the problem, and his self-esteem continued to deteriorate.

Finally, his dad was able to take him to a pediatrician for a full assessment. The doctor informed the dad that there was a physiological basis for the encopresis. Jamal was prescribed medication to loosen his bowels, and the doctor recommended a change in his diet. My client could have avoided his social isolation and the damage to his self-esteem had he been assessed by a pediatrician two months earlier.

Summary:

- Enuresis and encopresis can be devastating on a child's self-esteem and social functioning.

- A traumatic event can cause a child to have enuresis or encopresis; however, a child may display these symptoms during only moderately stressful situations as well.

- It's critical that you rule out physiological basis for these symptoms.

- If there's an emotional basis for the symptoms, individual and family therapy are recommended in order to address the root causes of the problem.

- Be matter-of-fact and non-shaming in relating to children with these problems.

Chapter 17

Children Who Lack
Age-Appropriate Social Skills

About 95% of the children I've worked with lack age-appropriate social skills. Often, they have no friends. Or if they have friends, they tend to be "negative." Some children have friends who are much younger than they are and have difficulty making friends with same-age peers. Others lack skills in developing and maintaining friendships. Some of the children I see are called "bullies" by other children, but most are called "sissies" or something much worse.

Children may lack appropriate social skills for various reasons. They may not have the opportunity to socialize outside of the home. Other children may lack social contact even in the school setting, because it is discouraged by their parents. Or perhaps the children feel too awkward associating with other kids outside of their home environment.

Lacking age-appropriate social skills can have far-reaching effects. A child's sense of self-esteem is definitely affected by lack of social skills and lack of friendships. We all have a need to be accepted by others and to belong to a group. When this need is not met, we feel socially and emotionally isolated and may lose touch with others and our community.

We hear about examples of how extreme social isolation pushes people over the edge. We hear about suicides and mass-shootings. But if a child is lacking in social skills, it doesn't necessarily mean that he will grow up to be a mass murderer. However, a child's self-esteem and his sense of self-efficacy will probably be affected by the lack of social skills. There is hope, however, because teaching your child social skills can be one of the easiest and most rewarding tasks for you and your child.

Case Study

I had a client who was 9 years old. Cindy's dad had sexually abused her when she was 6 years old. Although our ultimate goal in therapy was to work on her sexual abuse issues, she indicated that her priority was to make friends. During our third session, after we had already established some rapport, she looked at me desperately and said she didn't have any friends. She said, "All I ever wanted was just one friend. You are the only friend that I have, even though you're a grown-up."

I told Cindy that I would help her make other friends. I pulled out one of my therapeutic books. Because she was extremely controlling, I didn't *tell* her to read the book. I thought she would refuse or suggest something else. I flipped through the pages of *Every Kid's Guide to Making Friends* by Joy Berry. I was melodramatic in my interest in the book. A few minutes later, Cindy took over and said she wanted to take turns reading the book.

The book talked about different types of friendships and what kids could do to make and keep friends. We role played different skills. I volunteered to act out the "wrong ways," and she agreed to act out the "right ways" to make friends. After we finished reading the book, I told her she could practice what she learned "in real life." I assured her, "It really works. You'll see."

Cindy's social skills improved dramatically over the next several weeks. After about six weeks, we talked about how she was doing in school. She let me know that she was doing great in school. I also casually asked her if she had any friends at school. She replied, "Are you kidding? Everybody's my friend at school, at least everybody in my class!" I didn't mention that she didn't have any friends about six weeks ago. I simply said, "Good! They are lucky to have you as a friend because you make such a good friend!"

With younger children, you can be direct in teaching them how to make friends. An out-going 5-year-old might ask another child, "Would you like to be my friend?" If your child is an outgoing type, but just happens to be lacking some skills, you can teach him to approach other kids in this fashion.

However, if he is more shy and reserved, you can teach him to make friends by teaching him to share with other kids and to talk about things that other children are interested in. *Every Kid's Guide to Making Friends* makes such recommendations.

When teaching children appropriate social skills, you should include assertive communication and active listening skills. You can also teach them to make "I-statements" to express their feelings appropriately. Teaching children assertive communication skills is especially important for teenagers because they are more susceptible to negative peer pressure.

One way to help children resist negative peer pressure is by helping them increase their self-esteem. You can also teach them the basics of communicating assertively. They need to learn they can refuse others politely but that they can also be firm in their refusal.

For instance, in session, my clients and I used to role-play different situations in which they would use assertive communication skills. Sometimes, they would make up a situation and challenge me to use the skills they learned in therapy. Because I have worked largely with foster kids, I make a point to help them use these skills in standing up for their personal safety rights.

Case Study

Nine-year-old LaTisha was sexually abused by her dad. It was unclear if her younger sister, Tiffany, was sexually abused as well. However, Tiffany tried to kiss her older sister on the cheek repeatedly without her permission. She also tried to "sneak" a hug from LaTisha by surprising her. During the sibling session, LaTisha complained about these incidents.

I asked LaTisha, "What would you like for Tiffany to do instead?" She said, "Well, I want her to stop! At least, she should ask me first." I agreed with her and encouraged her to speak up for herself.

With my coaching, LaTisha was able to tell her sister, "Tiffany, I don't like it when you kiss me and hug me. I want you to wait until I say 'okay.' Anyway, you're supposed to ask me first." Tiffany apologized, and I praised Tiffany for apologizing. I also praised her sister for speaking up for herself.

Then, I asked them, "And what does it mean when people say they're sorry?" They both responded, "It means you're sorry, and you won't do it again." I praised them once again and encouraged them to practice what they learned in therapy.

During the subsequent sessions, when LaTisha tried to get me to intervene on her behalf, I matter-of-factly reminded her to stand up for herself when her sister "forgot" about respecting her boundaries. However, LaTisha eventually remembered to do this on her own, and Tiffany learned to ask for her sister's permission to hug her or to kiss her on the cheek.

In the above example, LaTisha used a very important communication skill called "using I-statements." You can teach a child to use I-statements in talking about her feelings and in using assertive communication. For instance, you can teach a young child to say, "I feel mad when you don't keep your promises. I would like for you to keep your promises."

With older adolescents, you can teach them to say, "I feel disappointed when you don't keep your word. Next time, please don't make any promises you can't keep." Of course, this means you better watch out and keep your own promises! If your children resort to using what you teach them, please do not argue with them. Praise them for speaking up for themselves, as long as it's done appropriately and respectfully. Then you can apologize and try to make amends, "I'll try to do better next time." It can be a wonderful opportunity for you to model for them how they should take responsibility for their actions!

In teaching children active listening skills, the most effective way is by modeling these skills. With younger kids, I tend to exaggerate my interest in hearing what they have to say. I look them in the eye, open my eyes slightly wide and nod occasionally, in order to encourage them to keep talking. When there's a pause, I may insert a question so they can clarify themselves, or I may encourage them to go on with their story.

With older children, I still make eye contact, but I try to be less melodramatic. I may nod occasionally or say, "Hmmm," "uh-huh," etc. With teenagers, again, it's very important not to assume things, make judgmental comments or make abrupt accusations. If a teenager says something that you disagree with or disapprove of, you may ask her to restate or clarify her statement.

Summary:

- The effects from lacking age-appropriate social skills can be far-reaching emotionally, as well as socially.

- Children may lack these skills for various reasons; however, you can teach them assertive communication and friendship skills through social skills training, modeling and role-playing.

- One way you can help children resist negative peer pressure is by helping them increase their self-esteem.

Chapter 18

Sibling Conflict

The issue of sibling rivalry has been talked about exhaustively over the past few years. But parents still talk about this because it continues to be a major issue for many children.

Children tend to have more fights or arguments with their siblings when they're bored. To counter this, I frequently recommend that the parents keep them busy. If a child has a problem keeping himself busy playing or doing a task with his siblings, you can tell him to keep busy alone.

As mentioned before, if young children fight over a certain toy, you can take it away and give them another chance to share the toy after a few minutes. If they fight over the toy a second time, they can have another chance to play with it the next day. If they have a problem the next day, they can find something else to play with for the next few weeks.

Or you can choose to separate them when they initially have a problem getting along with each other. You can separate them for a few minutes, just long enough for them to miss playing with each other.

To help my clients improve their relationship with their siblings, I often hold sibling sessions, in which I allow them to play together. Initially, I teach them to share and to take turns with each other. I also teach them to have patience and to encourage one another. I model for them how they can apologize and accept apology with grace.

Then, I let them play together to see what happens. Usually, they'll get along well, at least during the beginning of the session. However, they usually get into an argument over something minor. "He cheated," "She won't share the Barbie with me," etc. I tell them, "You guys handle it." Then, I pretend to be busy writing notes.

Sometimes, they can resolve the conflict on their own. However, if they continue to argue over the toy, I simply take it up. If one complains that the other is cheating, I may ask them how they think they can resolve the problem.

One time, I had a child respond, "Stop playing the game?" I was about to agree with him, but the other child said, "Okay! Okay! We can play by the rules." I told them that it was a great idea.

Case Study

I used to work with a parent who used to make his younger children sit together and hold onto each other's hands for five minutes every time they would get into an argument. They couldn't talk or hurt each other during this time. If they hurt each other, they received an additional consequence, much less pleasant than holding each other's hands.

They were able to cool down usually within the first couple of minutes. Their anger wouldn't last long. Often, the foster dad would hear them giggle and whisper to each other like they were best friends, their argument completely forgotten from a few minutes earlier.

Their dad was kind enough to explain to me what he was doing. This was his way of trying to teach them that the logical consequence for not getting along with each other was to be put in a situation in which they would have to get along with each other.

Another way to help children get along with each other is by allowing them to participate in recreational activities together. As they play together, you can praise them for cooperating, sharing, or taking turns with each other.

You can also praise them when they're helpful, encouraging or patient with one another. With younger children, you can give them rewards or privileges for getting along with their siblings. For example, if you see a child giving his last bite of ice cream to his younger brother, you can give him a bite of your ice cream. You can also pat the older one on the back and praise him for being such a good brother.

Sometimes when one child behaves positively, the other one behaves negatively, as if the latter is trying to compensate for his sibling's positive behaviors. In this case, I explain to both kids that everybody can be "good" at the same time.

I tell them, "Just because your mom tells your brother how good he is, that doesn't mean that you're bad. Both of you can be good at the same time. And you guys can do good things at the same time too."

You should refrain from comparing your children to each other. This can negatively effect both children's self-esteem. One child may think that he's not good compared to the other one. The other one may think that his mom won't love him unless he acts "good" all the time.

In therapy, I tell the older sibling to be a positive role model. However, instead of saying that he needs to be a positive role model for his younger brother, I tell him he needs to be a positive role model *for himself.* I explain, "And if your brother happens to benefit from what you do, well, that's good for him. But, you need to do what's right because you know it's the best thing for you." Then I explain to the younger sibling that he can be a positive role model for his older brother. I tell both of them that people need to be a positive role model for each other regardless of their age.

Having said all this, some researchers indicate that the more we focus on sibling rivalry, the worse it may get. The more a parent tries to intervene during a sibling conflict, greater may be the frequency or severity of conflicts.

This may be due to the fact that both children receive more attention from their parents when they're having the conflict.

Therefore, some therapists believe that parents should let kids just handle the conflict on their own. I agree with this to a certain point; parents should use common sense and intervene when it concerns their children's safety.

Summary:

- Children tend to have more fights or arguments with their siblings when they are bored.
- Use logical consequences in redirecting children during a sibling conflict.
- Give them a break from each other if they are unable to resolve the conflict on their own.
- Sibling therapy or family therapy may be necessary if the conflict is serious or chronic.
- Recreational activities can encourage children to get along with each other.
- Let children know that "everybody can be good at the same time" and that they don't have to be in competition with each other.
- A younger sibling can be a positive role model for his older sibling, just as the older sibling can be a positive role model for him.
- Focus attention away from the sibling conflict and acknowledge children when they do get along with each other.

Chapter 19

The Problem with Tattling

I haven't known a single child who hasn't tattled on another child. I've come to believe that tattling is part of being a kid. However, there are some that have a major problem with tattling. They go overboard and tattle on other children on just about everything. "Dad, Tommy's laughing at me." "Dad, Tommy's not doing his homework." "Dad, Tommy won't close his door." Enough already!

When a child tattles on another kid, I first ask her if she's trying to be helpful or hurtful. Children can be helpful when they inform us that another child has been hurt or if the other child is in danger. Otherwise, they usually tattle on others to get them in trouble. That's when they're being hurtful.

For example, if Janie says something negative about Dan, Janie has to say at least three positive things about Dan to neutralize her negative comments about him. I should require Janie to tell me seven positive things, since it takes this many positive comments to make up for one negative comment. But I only require her to say three positive things about the person she's tattling on. This still defeats her purpose, because instead of getting Dan in trouble, she ends up telling me how good he is.

Sometimes, children pretend they can't think of anything positive to say about the other person. In that case, I tell them to take their time and write down three positive things. This usually prompts them or motivates them to quickly come up with at least three things. With younger children, I usually end up helping them come with three positive things about their siblings. But it still proves to be effective in taking away their motivation for tattling on their sister or brother.

If Janie tells me something minor about Dan, I won't even address it with him, especially in front of Janie. I don't want to reward her for tattling on others. If what the she tells me is serious, and if she's trying to be helpful, I praise her for informing me about what's going on. I also praise her for looking out for Dan and for being concerned about him.

Chapter 20

Anxiety

Your child may have problems with anxiety if he or she exhibits the following symptoms:

- Avoids people, places or situations
- Bites her nails
- Pulls out her hair
- Picks on scabs or other injuries
- Has difficulty speaking out in class
- Has difficulty making and keeping friends
- Isolates herself from others
- Has obsessive thoughts
- Engages in compulsive behaviors
- Has nightmares
- Has problems with enuresis and/or encopresis
- Worries obsessively about past or current events or about possible future events
- Is hyperactive
- Is easily irritable or tired

- Has difficulty concentrating or focusing on tasks
- Has psychosomatic disturbances
- Has insomnia
- Hoards objects

Children become anxious for various reasons, from their parents' separation to their upcoming move to a different city. Adults often minimize their children's feelings because they cannot understand their children's reactions. However, as discussed earlier, it's important to validate their feelings first if you want to help them cope with their feelings.

Case Study

Eight-year-old Bailey was highly anxious after her parents' divorce. She believed that she caused the divorce because her parents argued about her frequently. And Bailey thought she wasn't a good girl and that this somehow caused her parents to divorce each other.

She tried to make up for her guilt by trying to be a perfect child around her mother, and tried to anticipate and fulfill her mother's needs, although she was only 8 years old. Her misunderstanding about the causes of her parents' divorce made her anxious about her behavior around her mother and father. Additionally, Bailey developed various psychosomatic illnesses. She often had stomachaches and headaches, which couldn't be explained by the school nurse. She was sent home on numerous occasions due to these symptoms, and her grades began to suffer.

In therapy, we processed about her parent's divorce. I clarified for her, in both individual and family therapy, the reasons for her parents' divorce. She learned to let go of her need to make things "okay" for her parents, and she eventually learned that it was not her responsibility to keep her parents together. Bailey started doing "normal" 8-year-old things, and she learned to play outside, hang out with her friends and worry about school (but on a normal level!).

When Your Child is Afraid of the Dark

Sometimes, parents worry if their child seems terrified of the dark. I had a 6-year-old client, Jorge, who was afraid of the dark. His dad told him that he was a "big boy" now and that he shouldn't be scared of the dark. After talking to the dad, we had a family session. During the session, we talked about how it's normal for all children to go through a stage in which they are afraid of the dark.

I talked about how children think there's a monster or a "boogieman" in the dark. Then, I admitted that I used to be fearful of the dark, until one day I stopped being scared. I explained to the children that it's okay for them to be afraid and that I was sure they would stop being scared of the dark one day too.

I stressed that there wasn't a set age in which children had to stop being scared, and that it varied from person to person. "Kids don't have to stop being scared just because they're older. They can stop being scared at any age. And that's okay." I told them that I stopped being scared when I was a teenager. I had such a good imagination that I would think of all kinds of monsters in the dark. Then I told them that I eventually learned that what I imagined wasn't real, just like I realized cartoons weren't real. I said, "And, you know, I'm pretty sure you're going to see that monsters and 'boogieman' aren't real either. And I have a feeling you're going to learn that pretty soon."

Nightmares

Children who are severely anxious sometimes have nightmares that can become terrifying even during their waking hours. With younger children, I try to validate their feelings first when they tell me about their nightmares. I then explain that they can actually have control over their dreams, by imaging how they want their dreams to be before they go to sleep. "This may not work when you first try it, but if you keep on picturing it in your mind— how you want your dreams to turn out—one day you'll have control over your dreams."

Case Study

I had an 8-year-old client named Emily who lived in a small group home for girls. She was sexually abused multiple times by multiple perpetrators. She said she had nightmares in which she saw her dad (one of the perpetrators) and the rest of her family drowning. A monster kept on trying to pull these people down into the water.

Fortunately, Emily had enough ego strength to see that she was the only person not drowning in the water. I validated how scared she must have felt in the dream. Then, I talked to her about controlling her dreams.

The following week, she told me she had the same dream again. However, this time, she was able to fight the monster as it was trying to drown her family. She became excited and told me that all the good guys from Pokemon helped her to fight the monster. The good guys "karate-chopped" the monster into pieces, and they were able to save all of her family, except for her dad. She said her dad drowned but that he went to Heaven where he got "better."

I wasn't sure if Emily really had this dream or if she had made it up. Either way, it was an opportunity for her to work through her feelings regarding her family, as well as her sexual abuse issues.

Naturally, I didn't ask her if her dream was real. Instead I mirrored her excitement and applauded her dream. I added, "I know that the good guys always win in the end! I just know it! Sooner or later, even if it's in Heaven, I know the good guys always win!" I told her this because she was still a child and because, in some ways, I still believe this in my heart.

I talked about heaven freely because she had mentioned it in her dream. I also added that I hoped God would help her dad get "better," so that he won't ever abuse another child again. Amy agreed with me, "Definitely!"

Anxiety and Obsessive Thoughts

Children can obsess over their family members or some event due to their anxiety. I had a 4-year-old client, Amy, who obsessed about her ex-foster mom for the first three months at her new placement. For a young child, this was a relatively long time to obsess over being separated from her ex-foster parents. However, Amy was in a unique situation because her ex-foster parents were supposed to adopt her. Unfortunately, the adoption did not go through.

Amy was especially bonded to her ex-foster mom, and the placement was disrupted rather abruptly due to an incident with another foster child in the home. During the sessions, Amy talked about her ex-foster mother, the ex-foster home, the toys at the home, etc. I allowed her to talk all she wanted about her ex-foster parents and other things pertaining to her prior placement.

I then slowly introduced other topics into the sessions, between our conversations about her ex-placement. I began redirecting her obsessive thoughts about her ex-foster parents. As the sessions progressed, I began inserting a little more conversation about her current foster parents. I asked her what she liked best about her current foster parents and her new family.

I asked Amy to draw a picture of her family. I did not clarify which family I wanted her to draw. Initially, she drew a picture of her ex-foster mom and herself. She left out her ex-foster dad and the other foster child. A few weeks later, I asked her to draw a picture of her family again. This time, she asked me which family I wanted her to draw. I knew that she still thought about her ex-foster parents, but she was gradually adjusting to her new home.

In order to help her adjust to her new home and stop obsessing about her ex-family, I asked her to draw a picture of her current family and added that I wanted her to draw everyone having fun with each other. After this session, she talked less and less about her ex-foster parents. She would occasionally call her ex-foster mother "Mom." She would then shake her head and clarify that she meant to say her "other mom."

I explained to Amy that it was okay for her to love her ex-foster parents and her current foster parents at the same time. I said, "You don't have to choose which one you like the best. You can love many people at the same time. The only thing different is that you're mom and dad you have now will be taking care of you. It's okay if you miss your other parents." I told her she could turn to her current foster parents when she misses her ex-foster parents, and encouraged her to talk to me as well during the sessions.

I suggested, "When you miss your other parents, you can go up to your mom and dad and tell them you're feeling sad because you miss your other parents. You can even ask them for a hug so you can feel better." After the session, I talked to Amy's current foster parents privately and coached them on how to respond to her when she seeks comfort from them.

Once she was given permission to talk openly about her feelings, she didn't obsess over the ex-foster parents as much as she did when she was first placed in her new home. As usual, it's when people try to negate our feelings or when they try to invalidate us that we feel more compelled to assert or act out our true feelings.

Anxiety and Compulsive Behaviors

Some children cope with their anxiety by engaging in compulsive acts. I had several younger clients who engaged in compulsive rituals in order to relieve their anxiety. During the sessions, they all displayed similar symptoms. Session after session, they would repeatedly line up the toys, perfectly parallel or vertical to the other toys. Often, they would become very frustrated if one of the toys either fell or got out of line somehow.

Initially in the session, I would help them set up the toys and go along with them, but I would then gradually redirect the session by having them talk about, rather than act out, their anxieties. I might say, "Boy, I can tell you're not feeling too happy with those dinosaurs. They just won't stay still, will they? You know, I can tell something's bothering you." At this point, my clients would usually tell me what has been bothering them.

At times, I might have to encourage my clients to open up during the session. "Tell me what happened today. I bet you have a very good reason to be upset." If they don't respond to open-ended questions such as these or my encouragement to elaborate,

I might ask more leading questions. "Did somebody do something or say something to make you upset today?" Or, "Are you upset about something that happened today?"

When a child first tells me about what happened, I often feel compelled to "fix" things for him to lessen his anxiety. My immediate reaction is to comfort him, rather than to actively listen until he finishes talking. Or I may forget to validate his feelings before I try to fix things for him.

It's amazing how I can help children lessen their anxiety just by listening to them and validating their feelings. I can actually see the relief on their face and the tension being released from their bodies. Sometimes, I may wait a while before I make recommendations or before I help them solve their problems.

Case Study

Recently, I had a 9-year-old client who was referred by a school counselor for his compulsive behaviors. Nathan was repeatedly late for his class because he would backtrack to the starting point if he couldn't walk to his class perfectly parallel or perpendicular to the hallway walls.

During the first session, I could tell he was anxious because he was very guarded and quiet. I had to do most of the talking as he dug up and lined up all the toys in the sandbox. He lined them up against the inside of the sandbox, all at an equal distance from each other.

His behaviors started to improve over the next couple of months. However, one day, his behavior regressed and he became very controlling during the session. He told me what to do and what not to do, and he became very frustrated when I didn't do exactly what he said.

I said, "Nathan, I can tell something's bothering you. Tell me what's going on. Did something happen today?" He told me his mom told him the night before that they would be moving again.

I first validated his feelings about the move. "It sounds like you're really upset about having to move again this year. Boy, I would feel upset too if I had to move so much."

Nathan responded, "Yeah, and I won't get to see my friends again. I'm not gonna have any friends at the new school. I told my mom I wasn't going to move, but she said I had to."

I encouraged Nathan to express his feelings. "Gosh, I wonder how I would feel if I had to start making friends all over again. By the way, how do you feel about not being able to see your friends again?"

He told me that he felt sad about it and added that he felt nervous about having to make new friends. I validated his feelings again and then asked him, "How did you feel when your mom told you that you *had* to move?" He said, "I felt mad. It's not fair we have to keep on moving every time she wants to. Why can't we just stay in one place for a while, like other people?"

I validated and expanded on his feelings. "It sounds like you're pretty upset that you can't have any say on whether or not you guys move. It'd be nice if you could stay in one place for a while, especially so you can be with your friends."

Nathan agreed with me and after our conversation he was significantly less controlling. He actually let me make-up some of the rules during the card game for the remainder of the session.

Stealing or Hoarding to Relieve Anxiety

Some children relieve their anxiety by stealing or hoarding things. The act is often compulsive and takes on characteristics of an addiction.

For instance, I worked with 11-year-old Steven about a year ago. He stole just about anything he could get his hands on; he stole pencils, walk-mans, extra pages from a coloring book, etc. He even tried to steal an extra piece of candy from me on a couple of occasions.

Although Steven stole compulsively, he apparently didn't want the stolen items as much as he did at the time he decided to steal them. He failed to benefit from most of the items. He would just collect them and store them under his bed and in his closet.

They were mostly little things, but they seemed to serve some purpose for him. After one of our sessions, I caught him trying to steal an extra piece of candy. When I confronted him about it, he laughed and said, "I was just joking. I was just trying to see if you were paying attention."

I laughed and then matter-of-factly told him to return both pieces to the candy box. He looked confused and asked me why he couldn't keep one of them, since he helped me clean up after the session. I explained to him that I wasn't sure if he didn't have a third piece.

I said, "Steven, it's difficult for me to tell when you're joking or when you're for real." I told him that when in doubt, I take people seriously. I continued, "When you joke around and pretend to take an extra piece of candy, I'm going to assume that you took an extra piece of candy, whether you did or not. Don't worry, Steven. You'll have another chance to get a piece of candy next time."

I then ended our conversation because I didn't want him to receive any more attention for his negative behavior. He tried to continue our conversation, but I told him that we didn't need to talk about it anymore and changed the subject.

As I mentioned previously, Steven had a problem with hoarding as well. I suspected that he was trying to relieve his anxiety about something. So, I met with his parents and recommended that they allow him to hoard things, as long as they were appropriate and as long as they weren't stolen property.

His parents stopped giving him attention and they stopped arguing with him about hoarding things. Eventually, he stopped hoarding things; it appeared as if he lost his motivation to continue these behaviors once his parents paid less attention to them. Steven moved on to collecting normal things, such as comic books, and he didn't hide them. He didn't have any reason to because they belonged to him.

I also recommended that his parents allow him to have some control over the minor things at home. I believe people feel anxious when they feel out of control or when they feel helpless. By providing Steven with some degree of control over his life, his parents were able to give him an outlet to relieve his anxiety.

Helping Anxious Children
to Problem-Solve

Often, children will come up with a very workable solution to their problems, even if they're only 4 years old. I try to allow children, teenagers especially, to come up with solutions as often as possible. Having them come up with the solutions increases the likelihood that they will follow through with their own advice. When we give out solutions freely, without encouraging them to come up with them on their own, they may see us as controlling and that we're just trying to tell them what to do. This is especially true if we try to fix things for them without their consent.

One of the most effective ways in which I've been able to help anxious children is by helping them to brainstorm different solutions. I praise them for their intelligence and creativity, and then I encourage them to try out one of their solutions. I remind them that if one doesn't work, they have plenty of other options.

In the above example, I might ask, "What do you think you can do next time something like this happens?" If my client has a problem coming up with possible solutions, I might suggest, "How about next time when you're taking a test and someone keeps on kicking you and bothering you, you raise your hand? Then you can tell the teacher what's going on. I'm not trying to tell you to get the other boy in trouble, but I'm trying to help you get him to leave you alone. That way you won't get into trouble for talking during a test."

Sometimes, children can add on to your suggestions or come up with a better idea. This is a perfect opportunity for you to become melodramatic and praise them for having such good ideas. You can increase his confidence by saying, "And I bet you'll take care of that problem from happening again!"

Children are very impressionable and can be easily influenced by how we respond to them. If we tell them that we bet something will work, they'll probably believe it wholeheartedly. This is especially true with younger children.

Naturally, teenagers are more sophisticated and skeptical. You may have to use a different approach with them. If one of my teenage clients is not ready or appears resistant to solving his problems, I might simply say, "You know, it looks like you got a real problem there. But I have a feeling you'll come up with a good solution." I might comfort him by lightly patting him on the back and then leave him alone. Sometimes, teenagers need some time and space to work things out for themselves. Or, at least, they need some time before they'll admit they need some help!

I tell parents that teenagers are supposed to be rebellious. According to Erik Erikson, one of the founding fathers of modern psychology, teenagers make it possible for our society to evolve by forcing us to see things and understand things from a new perspective. However, parents often believe that their teens are just being difficult or argumentative.

You can teach teenagers that it's okay to disagree with you and to have their own opinions without being argumentative or disrespectful towards you. Of course, the best way to teach them is through modeling. You can disagree with them and make your point without being disrespectful towards them.

Physical Activity to Relieve Tension and Anxiety

Anxious children can become highly restless and tense, so much so that they can't function in their day-to-day activities. In order to help alleviate these symptoms, I encourage them to release their anxieties through some form of physical activity. I also inform their parents, so they can help monitor their children's activities. Care must be taken if the child is under medical care or taking psychotropic medication.

Consult your child's pediatrician regarding appropriate activities and your child's level of involvement in these activities. Sometimes, you need to be cautious in exposing your child to sunlight if he's taking medication.

Many of the symptoms listed can be alleviated by your child's participation in sports. Walking just 20 minutes a day can help lessen the intensity of the symptoms. You can join in the walk, and it can become a great opportunity for you to bond with each other. Or, the whole family can join in and enjoy each other's company in a relaxed atmosphere.

Sometimes, children are more motivated to engage in physical activities if the activities are more competitive or active in nature. When I talk to my clients about getting rid of their worries by doing something active, they often get excited about playing basketball, football, baseball, etc.

Once, I had a 12-year-old boy tell me, with confidence and determination in his voice, that he could run around the house 10 times if he feels frustrated or mad. He said, "That should take care of it!" Naturally, I agreed with him, with just as much confidence.

Summary:

- Children become anxious for various reasons, from physical abuse to attending a new day care.

- Validate your child's feelings even if you disagree about how he should feel.

- A child may be anxious due to a misunderstanding.

- Problem-solving can help teach anxious children to cope with the root causes of their problems.

- An anxious child may display psychosomatic symptoms, such as headaches and nausea.

- Individual and family therapy are recommended for children with anxiety or other anxiety-related problems.

- An anxious child may engage in obsessive thoughts or compulsive behaviors.

- Some children hoard or steal things in order to relieve their anxiety. You can use logical consequences in these situations.

- Give children as much control as possible over the minor things in their lives in order to lessen their anxiety.

- Some children may regress under stressful situations and have nightmares or become afraid of the dark. A child therapist can help them process their feelings and find creative coping mechanisms.

- Encourage your kids to participate in physical or recreational activities to relieve their anxiety.

Chapter 21

Separation Anxiety

A child may have problems with separation anxiety if she displays the following symptoms. Please note that if the child has only one or two of the symptoms, she may not have a problem with separation anxiety. Usually, she must exhibit most of these symptoms for a certain length of time to be diagnosed with this problem.

- Cries or has tantrums when separated from her parents or other caretakers
- Worries excessively about being separated from her parents
- Avoids going to school or other places outside of the home
- Has psychosomatic symptoms prior to the separation or during the separation
- Tries to find excuses to sleep near her parents
- Worries excessively about the caretaker's welfare during her separation (for example, she may worry that her mother might get into a car accident)
- Follows her parents around the house almost constantly
- Unable to fall asleep without her parents' presence

A child can develop separation anxiety for various reasons, such as the death of a family member, parental divorce, etc. Often the symptoms can be so severe that parents are unable to perform simple tasks around the house without being interrupted by the child. She can be clingy and have tantrums when her parents try to leave her, even for a brief period, to another part of the house.

Case Study

I had a 4-year-old client, Moses, who had problems with separation anxiety. Moses began to show these symptoms shortly after his parents were separated. According to his mother, he would cry for hours until he got what he wanted, and he would try to follow her around the house at all times.

He even had tantrums if he couldn't follow her into the restroom. She had to resort to covering herself with a towel while she was using the restroom. Moses refused to go to sleep unless he was in his mother's bed. Because the mother needed to get her sleep, she gave in and allowed her son to take over her life.

I believe she allowed him to do these things because she felt guilty about the separation from his father. When she dropped him off at his daycare, he had severe tantrums and cried unceasingly, while she tried to comfort him and plead with him to let her go.

After the initial assessment, I recommended individual and family therapy for both the mother and the son. During the individual sessions, I was able to process how Moses felt about his parents' separation. He was resistant in the beginning, but eventually he was able to talk openly about how he felt about being separated from his dad. Moses' mother had suspected sexual abuse by his father and had taken legal measures to suspend the visitations.

He was also able to play out his fears and nightmares during play therapy. I also consulted with his mother individually. I asked her to allow Moses to gradually get used to the idea of being separated from her. I recommended that she occupy his attention with other children or with his favorite toy or TV show.

She began leaving Moses in the living room for approximately three minutes to go into the kitchen. The house was designed so that he was able to see her in the kitchen. She matter-of-factly carried on conversations with him and then came back into the living room and praised him for playing so well.

Using this approach, she was able to leave him in the living room or his room, while she was completely out of his sight for three minutes. She gradually increased the time by two-minute increments.

Moses still had difficulty falling asleep without her presence. So she performed household chores, like folding the laundry, in her son's room as he tried to fall asleep. After a few days, she moved onto paying the bills or writing letters. She shortened their conversations as she pretended to be busy with her tasks, but she intentionally tried to make some noise, so that he would know she was still near him. Moses began to fall asleep more readily as he felt more secure of his mom's presence. She had purchased a baby monitor so she could hear him in case he would wake up in the middle of the night. She would immediately go into his room and pretend to write letters until he would fall asleep again.

During the consultation, his mother reported that she could hardly get any sleep or accomplish anything around the house. Understandably, she complained that she couldn't do anything for herself because she was too busy meeting her son's emotional needs.

However, after about three weeks, she reported a significant decrease in her son's level of anxiety. She said that he still had episodes where he would refuse to part from her, but that he was now able to go to bed without her being in the room or around his room.

She explained that he would call out for her immediately after going to his room and talk to her, probably to make sure that she was still in the house. She had to leave a nightlight on in his room and get him a special "Mama Bear" to protect him at night.

At his daycare, she learned to break away from Moses as soon as possible. After talking briefly to the daycare worker to exchange information, she would let him know that she was leaving. Then, she would quickly give him a hug and a kiss, and let him know she would be picking him up after work, as she left the daycare center. Initially, the daycare worker reported that his tantrums became more severe. However, after only three days, he stopped having the tantrums altogether and was able to join the other children in their morning activities.

I recommended that when she picks up her son promptly at 5:30 every evening, she praise him and ask him about his activities for the day. I asked her to give her full attention as he talked about his day and to be enthusiastic in her responses. She praised him about how smart he was getting in "school" and how well he was playing with the other children. She also told him, "Now, make sure you remember all the fun stuff you do tomorrow at school, so you can tell me about them when I pick you up." This helped Moses to look forward to his next day at daycare. It also indirectly reminded him that she would be back to pick him up from the daycare center.

I cautioned his mother to be very consistent about her pickup time. If she's late by 30 or even 15 minutes, he could regress to exhibiting some of the symptoms again. His level of anxiety could actually increase from this one incident. Because he was only 4 years old, Moses would not have understood the reasons for her lateness. Although he may lack the concept of time, he would have been aware that his mom was late, because the other children would have gone home by the time she got there 30 minutes late.

Separation anxiety can last a relatively short time, or it can last years on into adulthood. Based on my experience, the prognosis is better if the child is treated as early as possible. And as in the above example, it takes patience and creativity on the parent's part to help her child through this difficult time.

Some of the symptoms of separation anxiety can be effectively resolved using proper approaches. One of the most important things a parent can do is to validate the child's experience and his feelings. If a parent dies, it is understandable if the child becomes anxious about the other parent's eventual death, even though there's no immediate threat.

Sometimes it makes matters worse if an adult tries to reason with the child. The child's fear may not be grounded in reality, and it may not be a rational response. Anxiety comes from our fears, and sometimes it's hard to make sense out of our feelings. Our behaviors and thoughts can result from our fears. As adults, we can learn to rethink our thoughts in order to fight these fears. However, with children, especially with the younger ones, this task is difficult due to their cognitive limitations.

Allowing the child to express his feelings and then validating his feelings may be the best approach. This does not mean that you are encouraging him to respond irrationally. What you are trying to do is let him talk about his feelings, so that you can validate his feelings. Let him know that you understand how he feels and that his feelings are okay (even though they may not be grounded in reality).

For instance, you can respond, "Bobby, I can tell that you're really scared and worried about me. And I know that's because you love me, just like I love you. When Mommy's not around you, she doesn't want anything to happen to you either. I think that you're worried about me because Daddy's in the hospital. I'm worried about him too. And I hope he gets better."

"But you know, Daddy's in the hospital because he's really sick. But Mommy's not sick. Do you remember the other day when you got sick and you threw up? Well, just because you got sick that didn't mean that Mommy had to get sick, right? So that means that just because Daddy's sick, it doesn't mean Mommy's going to get sick."

"I tell you what. When you get worried about Daddy or Mommy, why don't you come tell me about how you're feeling? And I'll give you a big hug, and we can talk about it. And you don't have to go on worrying about what's going to happen to us all by yourself. But you have to remember to come to Mommy and talk about it right away when you start worrying about us. Okay?"

Summary:

- A child may develop separation anxiety for various reasons, from the death of a family member or his parents' divorce.

- Children may exhibit severe tantrums as a result of this problem; you should use a child-centered approach with these children.

- Parents can desensitize their child by gradually getting him accustomed to being separated from them.

- Parents should validate their child's feelings and try to refrain from reasoning with him.

Chapter 22

School Problems

Children often exhibit academic or behavioral problems in school as a result of problems at home or with friends, or because of some other emotional problems. I want to address this issue, if only briefly, because this problem is so prevalent in our society.

These problems often improve or disappear entirely when the underlying issues are addressed. Children may have school problems because of depression or their reaction to parental divorce. In these instances, they can turn to their therapist, their parents or other adults in order to process their feelings about these matters.

Problems in Learning

At times, children have problems in school due to unidentified learning disorders or due to some physiological reasons. Your child may have problems with her vision or hearing but neglect to tell you about it. Or she may have problems with dyslexia.

Example

I had a friend whose dyslexia wasn't diagnosed until he was 20 years old. He was struggling in college and had to spend countless hours in tutoring just to get by until he was a junior in college. He said he had problems with reading even when he was in grade school but that he didn't know he had dyslexia at that time.

He thought that he wasn't as bright as the other children in his class and that he just needed to work harder to get through school. His self-esteem naturally suffered as a result, and it was evident to me that he still couldn't shake off this image of himself. He still feels he doesn't quite measure up to his peers and still has a low opinion of himself.

If a child is behind academically, especially in reading or other fundamental subjects, it may be a good investment to have her tested by a psychologist. As always, when you find the root causes for a particular problem, you're better equipped to solve the problem or take measures to compensate for the problem. In my friend's case, he compensated by seeking tutoring and studying harder than most of his peers. It took him a year longer than he planned, but he eventually graduated with a BS in mechanical engineering. He is now a successful engineer in a major computer-based company.

Special Education

Sometimes children need to be placed in a special education setting for either academic and/or emotional problems. A few of the children I worked with actually developed more problems when they were first admitted into these classes. However, most of them were eventually able to adjust to the setting, as well as their new teachers and rules.

With children who continue to have difficulty in this setting, parents must weigh the pros and cons of keeping their child in special education. This setting may have its drawbacks, but sometimes parents realize that this is what their child needs. Of course, the child often doesn't have a choice but to attend special education because of school policies (unless his parents opt for home schooling).

I used to make school visits, usually to smaller schools out in rural areas. One of the schools that I went to had paint peeling off the buildings and had an office that had been converted literally from a storage closet. But of the schools I have had the privilege of visiting, it is one of my favorite schools.

The school staff welcomed visiting therapists and just about anybody else who was interested in helping their children. They even had a special education teacher who was also a foster parent and a licensed therapist. The teacher had an open door policy with the visiting therapists and kept a very flexible schedule.

He explained that he wanted to make himself available to us, because in the long run, it would make his job easier. He said he understood that if his students could receive help for their emotional problems, then they would be able to function better in his class. With our combined efforts, we were able to help several of his students mainstream back into regular classes throughout the school year. That's putting our tax dollars to work!

Content Mastery Classes

In Texas, some of the children who do not meet all of the qualifications for "special education" have access to Content Mastery. In Content Mastery, teachers help students with their work if they need more help or guidance than what is available in their regular classes.

Different schools use Content Mastery differently. Many of my clients, especially in smaller rural schools, had the freedom to go into their content mastery classes whenever they felt overwhelmed by the work in their regular classes. Although these classes are not 100% effective, most of my clients benefited from having this option.

School Problems Due to Lack of Motivation

Often, children have academic difficulties in school not because they're intellectually lacking, but because they lack motivation. For teenagers, their friends are often their top priority. Often, they push aside their family, as well as their schoolwork, to hang out with their friends or to fit in with their peers. Although their parents know that this is "normal" for their age, it still makes it difficult to stand by and watch them fail in school.

Example

I have a friend who has a 15-year-old son. Recently, I stayed at her house on an extended vacation in Colorado. My friend's son and I got a chance to get to know each other well, as we watched movies and as he taught me about kayaking and fly-fishing.

One evening, I was watching a sitcom with my friend, her husband and their son. After the show, the son commented, "I guess I better get to reading and do my homework." My friend responded, "I think that might be a real good idea."

It turned out that he was taking summer school because he had failed his history class. He thought history was boring, so he guessed his answers on most of the assignments and tests during the regular school year. He pointed out that sometimes he made A's or B's just by guessing. I admitted that I used to guess sometimes when I was in school, although not all the time.

I then innocently asked him, "Hey, why don't you just keep on guessing?" His parents looked at me like I was crazy. While he wasn't looking, I winked at them. Their son responded, "Yeah, I did, but I got a 65 on my last assignment, and I need to pass this class." I said, "Yeah, that's what bites about guessing. Sometimes you get lucky and sometimes you don't." His parents looked at me with relief on their faces.

The next morning I saw their son working on another assignment. We had a little chitchat, and then he showed me why it was difficult to guess his answers sometimes. Once again, I innocently asked him, "Why don't you just guess the answers and then look them up later to see how many you guessed right. It is an open book assignment, isn't it? If you get good at guessing, maybe you'll get by just by guessing."

Once again, he told me he was good at guessing. He said, "It's because I'm good at ruling things out." I responded, "Well, that's because you're smart. You're good at making *educated* guesses. But, check this out. The funny thing is, if you didn't actually learn something in school already, you wouldn't be able to make educated guesses. If you had guessed all your life, how much do you think you would know by now?"

His eyes widened in comprehension, and he replied, "Zero?" I said, "Well, I don't know about that, but you wouldn't know much. That's for sure." I told him to have fun studying and then walked away.

Instead of telling him what he should do, I tried to make him think and come up with his own lesson for the day. Sometimes using this approach can prove to be more effective than long, drawn-out lectures.

Summary:

- Children often exhibit academic or behavioral problems in school due to problems at home.

- Children may display these symptoms due to problems in learning (such as dyslexia).

- Children may need to be placed in content mastery or special education in order to meet their academic and/or emotional needs.

- Sometimes a child may have school problems due to lack of motivation; using logical consequences can help to address this problem.

Chapter 23

Children with Low Self-Esteem

Many children suffer from lack of self-esteem. They are bombarded by what's "ideal" in the media, and they're almost constantly criticized by their peers about their appearance. Whatever the root cause, lack of self-esteem can have a detrimental effect on their emotional well-being.

Responding to Children with Low Self-Esteem

Children make statements that put down their worth, accomplishments or abilities. Even in children who tend to be self-centered, I often hear such negative statements. Instead of saying, "No! You're not dumb," I may respond, "I can tell you're not feeling too good about yourself. What happened today?"

The first statement merely negates the child's experience, as well as her feelings. In the second response, I am not agreeing with her that she's dumb, but I'm letting her know that I heard what she said and I understand what she's feeling now. But I go a step further and give her an opening or an option to share more about why she's feeling so bad about herself that day. It may be that she tripped over something during one of her classes and almost fell in front of her peers. Or, it may be that her art teacher criticized her work in front of the whole class. In the first scenario, you can respond, "Uh-oh, that could be kind of embarrassing. But I'm glad you didn't fall." She could respond, "Yeah, that would have been worse!" Then, you can comfort her by gently patting her on the back and move on to another subject.

In the second scenario, you could respond in the following manner:

Parent: *Boy, I wonder how I would have felt if my teacher did that in front of the whole class! How did you feel when he did that?*

Teen: *Well, kinda stupid. He made fun of my work in front of everybody!*

Parent: *Yeah, I would have felt pretty bad too. That is, until I get to thinking about what he did. Now, I would think, as teacher, he could have been a little bit more sensitive and encouraging to his students. What is the deal there? What did he say about your artwork anyway?*

Teen: *Well, he didn't say exactly there was anything wrong with my picture. But I couldn't say anything because I was so embarrassed. He picked on my work when he could have talked about anybody else's.*

Parent: *I can tell you're still feeling pretty bad about what happened. It sounds like you don't even want to go back to his class.*

Teen: *Yeah, I wish!*

Parent: *Yeah. That would be nice. But both of us might get into trouble! You for skipping your class, and me for encouraging it! Well, what do you think you could do to resolve this problem?*

Teen: *Well, I guess I can tell him to go to you-know-where," but I guess that won't do any good. I guess I can go up*

to him tomorrow before the class starts and ask him what
he thought was exactly wrong with my picture. Maybe I
didn't understand the assignment.

Parent: *Hmmm, I think that's a great idea.*

How Perfectionism Effects
Children's Self-Esteem

I rarely work with perpetrators of abuse. However, I recently
had a client that came to see me because the court mandated that
he receive at least six sessions on anger management skills. He
had to learn these skills before the court would allow his children to move back home from their foster placement.

On the third session, he finally realized that his children
didn't have to be perfect and that playing was just as important
for kids as it was for them to make good grades in school or for
them to behave well at home. He became teary-eyed and told
me that he used to expect them to be perfect and get angry with
them if everything wasn't "just so" with their clothes, their
rooms, etc.

He then talked about the way his father raised him. His father wanted him to be perfect. Again, he became teary-eyed and
expressed regret for having unrealistic expectations from his children. He cried and said, "Man, I probably did what my dad did
to my self-esteem. And I feel like crap!" He said he didn't want
his kids to grow up like him and that he wanted them to be happy
and learn to play "and not miss out on their childhood."

We all need to remember to be loving, kind, patient and for-
giving with children. It's very difficult to love anyone unconditionally. However, we must make our best effort to love children
unconditionally if we want their self-esteem to remain intact.

Physical Characteristics
and Self-Esteem

I had an 8-year-old client named Julian. He was a premature
baby and still very small for his age. When he was very young,

people thought he was cute. However, as he grew older and as his peers began to tower over him, he became very self-conscious about his height.

When I first started seeing Julian, I thought it might be an issue for him, but he didn't say anything about his size or his height until our fourth session. I asked him what he would wish for if he could have any three wishes. Julian indicated that he would like to be "just a little bit bigger."

We then started working on this issue. I knew that his self-esteem suffered from being so short compared to his friends. In fact, he told me that his friends made fun of him because of his height. He complained that they called him names. I responded, " It makes you feel pretty bad when other kids make fun of you, doesn't it?"

He nodded his head in agreement. I continued, "You know why I think they make fun of you?" Before he could answer, I said, "It's because they haven't heard about the little boy who saved his whole village."

"The little boy just happened to see the water coming out of the hole, as he was passing by the dam one evening. There was no one else around. He yelled for help, but nobody heard him. Well, he stayed there all night, with his little pinkie in the dam. The villagers found him still sitting by the dam early next morning."

I told my client, "And because he was little and had a pinkie just the right size, he saved the whole village and became a hero. If it wasn't for the little boy's pinkie, the hole would have gotten bigger and bigger and the dam would have eventually burst, drowning everybody in the village." By the end of the story, I could tell from his facial expression that he was impressed with the story.

Several weeks later, he came into the session, all excited, and told me about playing football with his friends. He said he was "small enough" to crawl under the other guy's legs to get away from him and make a touchdown. He exclaimed, "He couldn't catch me!" Naturally, I joined in the excitement and applauded him. He said, "It pays to be small sometimes." I agreed with him.

How Praising Effects
Children's Self-Esteem

My favorite way to help children with low self-esteem is by praising them generously. As discussed earlier, praising is a powerful way to influence their behavior. A positive side effect in praising children is that it not only increases their self-esteem but also their sense of self-efficacy. They feel they can do just about anything!

When you observe a child engaging in a positive behavior, praise him generously. With very young children, you really can't "overdo it" with praises. However, with your teenagers, you may need to tone down the praises, especially in front of their friends. One-on-one, I can tell they love praises just as much as my younger clients. But, for some reason, teenagers get all embarrassed in front of their friends! Even with teenagers, I try to touch them at least briefly, in some positive way, so I can let them know that I really appreciate them.

When you praise children repeatedly, you can't help but to influence their self-esteem in positive ways. You should recognize them for doing things that you normally expect teenagers to do (such as, doing their homework or their part of the household chores). Or, you can praise them for doing something above and beyond on their own initiative (such as helping their younger sister with her homework).

When I hear a child making negative statements about the way she looks or about her lack of intelligence, I try to remember not to negate what she says immediately. Although I never agree with her, I try to allow her to talk about how she feels about herself and why she feels that way.

If she says she's a smart girl, I agree with her and praise her for being smart enough to know that she's smart. If she says she feels dumb, I validate her feelings but also ask her, "What made you say that?" I ultimately try to get my clients to talk about their feelings.

In praising children, it's important for you to remember not to base your praises solely on what they're able to perform. A child's self-esteem should not be performance-based exclusively. In helping her realize her sense of worth, you should let her know that she's special and worthy just the way she is.

Example

My friends have three beautiful, "thriving" children. All of the kids are extremely intelligent, considerate and creative. Every time I went to visit them, my friends would get excited and have their kids perform a new talent they learned recently.

I could tell they loved their kids and were very proud of them. I think parents should let their children know when they are proud of them. In therapy, I regularly brag about my clients in front of their parents. I learned that when I praise children in front of an adult, it has three times the power than if I were to praise them without another adult's presence.

I didn't have anything against how proud my friends were of their daughters. They had a good reason to be. However, one day, I saw the oldest daughter roll her eyes back when her mother told her to show me what she learned to play on the piano a few days prior to my visit. My friend didn't see this, and I decided to pretend that I didn't see it either.

My friend's daughter played the piano, even though I could tell she wasn't that excited about performing in front of me. Later that evening, the daughter and I talked about cartoons and school, and we also got around to talking about her piano lessons.

I told her, "It's neat how you can play the piano, paint beautiful pictures and how you're so smart in school. But, you know what, I bet you're neat even when you're just watching cartoons or just having fun with your friends." She looked shocked, and she didn't respond for a few seconds. And then she smiled, and we continued our little chitchat.

Several weeks later, her parents gave me a surprise birthday party. Their daughter made me a homemade birthday card. It was my first homemade card since I was about 10 years old. In it, she told me that I was her "best grown-up friend." We've been friends ever since.

Summary:

- Many children suffer from lack of self-esteem due to various reasons.

- Validate their feelings and refrain from telling them how they should feel about themselves; instead, listen to children to get to the root causes of their inadequate feelings.

- Genuine and specific praises can help boost children's self-esteem; however, praises should not be solely performance-based.

- Perfectionism and uncommon physical characteristics can effect a child's self-esteem negatively; parents should be realistic in their expectations and they should redefine their children's characteristics in positive terms to help counter the negative effects.

Chapter 24

Special Issues Related to
Therapeutic Parenting

Ethics and Children

With children, the terms "confidentiality" and "limits to confidentiality" usually have a different meaning than for the adult clients. With foster kids, as well as "biological" kids, I have often found it therapeutically necessary to keep their parents informed about the significant issues during the sessions.

For instance, if a child makes a statement about wanting to run away or wanting to hurt himself, I inform my client's parents for his safety. For this reason, I always make a point of explaining to my young clients about the limits to confidentiality during the initial session.

I tell them that although our sessions are private, there's a limit to their privacy when it comes to their safety. I also leave room for other important issues by indicating that I may need to talk to their parents about other "important things" for their well-being.

With teenagers, I try to respect their privacy. If a teenager finds out that I've been sharing everything with his parents, he may not be as open with me during our subsequent sessions. Some therapists believe that they should always inform their teenage clients if they're about to share some information with their parents. However, I believe this to be counter-therapeutic in some situations. For example, since teenagers sometimes have a tendency to do exactly the opposite of what adults suggest, I often recommend that their parents use a technique that's commonly referred to as "reverse psychology." If I tell my clients about my intention to use this approach, it would defeat the purpose.

Case Study

Marisa was scheduled to graduate from high school a couple of months after I started seeing her. However, towards the end of school, she said she changed her mind about going to college. Marisa wanted to take a break from school and make some money.

Instead of arguing with her, I said, "Well, if that's what you really want, I think you should. Hey, maybe this is a chance for you to make lots of money and save up. Maybe you can get two jobs working at McDonald's and at Taco Bell or at Walgreen. They're all within walking distance, and since you don't have a car, it'll be easy for you to get to work."

Marisa was hoping that she might work at Dillard's out at the mall and that her parents could take her to work. She wanted to work at a place a little more glamorous than McDonald's, Taco Bell or Walgreen. After our session, she had second thoughts about putting off college, and she eventually decided to go to college right after high school.

If I had told Marisa that I intended to tell her parents to use a similar approach, I would have defeated my purpose of redirecting her. She would have known that "we were all in on it" to encourage her to attend college, and then she probably would have made it clear to us that she intended to do exactly what she pleased, without our interference.

A note of caution: When using this approach, only make suggestions that won't backfire on you. You should be fairly confident of your teenager's response, because there's always a danger that she may agree with you and actually go along with your suggestions!

Children's Rights

Children have rights too. Our society is becoming more aware of their needs and their rights as individuals. I believe, as a nation, we are lagging behind some of the other developed countries in advocating for children's rights.

Although this may be the case, I also believe measures can be taken to correct this situation. While waiting for laws to pass, we can still treat children as individuals and with respect. We should advocate for them, whether they're our children or our neighbor's children. It's time that we treat children as our community's responsibility, and not just their immediate family's responsibility. It's a critical time for us to realize this, especially when our society is faced with the astounding number of children who are abused each year.

We can advocate for children through our legal system and through our school system. We can advocate for them professionally, and we can advocate for them personally in our homes. As children grow older, I believe they need to exercise more choices and freedom, because this ultimately leads them to accept more responsibility.

Children should be allowed to vote during the family meetings about household chores or other minor issues. From this process, they can learn they have a right to their opinions and a right to express what they think is fair or unjust. Once they reach adulthood, hopefully, they can apply what they've learned and exercise their right to petition for what they believe in.

Working with the Legal System

Whether you're a biological parent or a foster parent, you may have to work with the legal system at some point. You may need to advocate for a child in case of abuse or help your child in case he becomes involved in illegal activities.

As we all know, our legal system isn't flawless, and it can be extremely frustrating to work with the system at times. However, for the children's welfare, it's important to remember to work with the system and not *against* the system.

You can speak up for children and try to protect them from the pitfalls in our legal system. However, as my favorite boss once told me, the court doesn't have to determine that a child was abused for you to believe the child.

If your child is called to court, you can help by preparing her emotionally for the court appearance. If she's in therapy, the therapist can help facilitate this process. If your child isn't in therapy, there are organizations such as CASA (Court Appointed Special Advocate) that can help.

Some courts also have a program that takes children on courtroom tours. They even allow the children to sit in the judge's chair and in the jurors' section to help them get used to the idea of being in the courtroom when it's their time to appear in court.

When I worked at Rape Crisis, part of my job description was to accompany my clients on these field trips. My job wasn't to coach them in what they should say in court but to inform them of the legal process as it relates to their case and to help them process their feelings about going to court.

Foster Parenting

As I was doing research for this book, I read several journal articles that proved to be supportive of my professional experience. Some of them discussed various approaches to parent training, and others addressed what characteristics accounted for effective parenting.

The articles also talked about foster parenting and what variables accounted for foster parents' satisfaction, as well as their effectiveness, in their role as caretakers. Some of the work addressed why some parents decide to discontinue fostering children.

Providing Male and Female Role Models

Children tend to do better when there are both a male and a female role model in the family. Research also indicates that children who grow up in single-parent families are more likely to be involved in crimes or other anti-social activities. This is distressing in light of the current rate of divorce and single-parent families.

However, even if a child lives in a single-parent family, this does not mean that he can't have access to positive male or female role models. There's no shortage of such models in our communities, our history and probably in the child's life, if we look hard enough. Your child could look up to his teacher, his uncle or even his "big brother," as long as they are people you would like your child to imitate. While there is a shortage of research on single-parent families headed by males, I believe that it's equally important to provide positive female role models for boys and girls.

If a child is in a single-parent family, he or she has access to numerous organizations and agencies that can provide positive male and female role models. These agencies include Big Brothers-Big Sisters, YMCA, YWCA, and numerous organizations where children can receive assistance or volunteer their services.

Single-Parent Foster Families

Although most foster homes tend to be two-parent households, there are some foster homes that are headed by single parents. If a foster dad is absent because he's stationed somewhere overseas, the foster child is essentially living in a single-parent home. Sometimes, children live in single-parent families due to a divorce prior to their placement.

Case Study

I had two teenage clients living in a single-parent home. One was 17 years old, and the other was about to turn 18 years old. This family was one of the most well-functioning families I've ever worked with compared to some other families.

The boys were fairly high functioning, although they still had therapeutic needs. The foster dad was also very skilled in using logical consequences and allowed them to learn from their own mistakes. The two boys responded to this approach very well and learned to be very self-sufficient. They even had jobs and maintained fairly high grades.

Case Study

In another single-parent home, however, the children's placement broke down after about six months. The foster mom initially had only one child placed in the home, and he was relatively easy to raise as long as he was the only child.

The foster mom was new to fostering children, and she had been a parent for less than a year. She appeared to be adjusting well to her new role; therefore, the child placement agency decided to place two more boys in the home.

Obviously, having one child in the home is different than having three children in the same home. The family dynamics changed almost overnight, and things proved to be a little bit overwhelming for the mom. The three boys' placement broke down, and the foster mom decided to stop fostering.

Research indicates that many foster homes close down within their first year for a myriad of reasons. In the above example, two of the children were teenagers. The family lived in a small community in which the mom felt isolated from other foster parents. There was also a lack of resources for the three boys in their community.

I believe this family could have worked out had there been another caretaker in the home, whether male or female. Part of the reason why the mom felt she couldn't handle the boys was because she couldn't stop them from horse playing and hurting each other.

Multi-racial Families

Many of the foster families that I've worked with had a mixture of different races, between the children themselves or between the parents and their foster children. Based on my experience, I think there are both pros and cons to having such families.

My ideal foster family includes children from many different ethnic backgrounds living in an exciting, multi-racial, multi-cultural household. However, in some families, this could prove to be counter-therapeutic for everyone.

Case Study

One foster home I worked in had a Mexican mother and an African-American father. The foster child that was placed in this home was a 17-year-old Anglo girl with a 6-month-old Anglo infant.

There are differences in the way different cultures raise their children. The girl and her baby didn't stay long in this family. The girl explained, "We just didn't click." It was a complicated situation that involved more than their racial differences. However, I believed race and culture did play a part in them not "clicking" with each other.

There are definite benefits to mixing children from different races or ethnicity. It gives them an opportunity to be not just tolerant, but also accepting of others who are different from them. In fact, I think it's a great opportunity for foster parents to teach children to appreciate and celebrate each other's differences.

In homes where there are primarily Anglo kids, I often recommend to the parents to encourage their African-American or Hispanic children to explore and celebrate their heritage. However, I don't endorse forcing these children to identify with their racial or ethnic background if they don't want to.

Case Study

I had a 12-year-old client, Maria, who didn't like Mexican boys. Her father had sexually abused her, and since he was Mexican she decided that she didn't like any Mexican or Hispanic-looking boys. Maria preferred "black" or "white" boys instead. I respected her choice, although I believed her reasons for avoiding Hispanic boys wasn't really healthy.

As a therapist, I'm supposed to respect my clients' rights to self-determination. However, I'm also bound to respect people from all racial and ethnic backgrounds.

I didn't tell Maria what she should do. I merely talked to her about what I believed about people in general. I told her that I believed everyone was essentially good, whether they're of African, Anglo, Hispanic or Asian descent.

I said, "I think this world would be a pretty boring place if it only had one kind of people in it. Just as all the colors in the rainbow make it beautiful, having people from all different races and all different backgrounds makes this world a beautiful and an interesting place."

I don't know if I did the right thing in telling her about what I believed, but I was honest and genuine in what I said. I don't believe that was the wrong thing to model for my client.

I saw her for a couple of years. By the end of the second year, she still preferred African-American or white boys, but she dated a couple of Hispanic boys at school. She broke up with them, not because of their ethnicity, but because of other reasons girls typically break up with their boyfriends over.

Case Study

I had another client who was a 16-year-old Anglo living in an African-American household. Bill moved into the home a year ago, and he became so bonded to his foster dad that he wanted to be black instead of white.

He associated with his African-American and Puerto Rican peers, but had no Anglo friends. He talked like his friends, he walked like his friends, and he dressed like his friends. In fact, in one of our sessions, he put down his race and talked about how "they" were no good.

I knew his foster parents well, and I highly doubted that he got these ideas from them. Bill was very angry with both of his biological parents, and I believe this was his way of separating himself from the pain he felt surrounding his parents. In one of our sessions, I told him so, and surprisingly he agreed with me. I validated and normalized his feelings, but I halfway jokingly told him, "I hope I don't tick you off. I don't want to be responsible for you hating Asians from now on." He smiled and assured me that this wouldn't happen.

I told him he was missing out on some of the best people in the world. I pointed out there are a lot of people from all different races and backgrounds who do terrible things to their children.

However, I also stressed that most people, even "white people," were good and descent under favorable circumstances. I told him, "After all, look at you. You're white, and you're not too bad!" He agreed with me.

Small vs. Large Families

Some families have up to eight or ten children. Although many people think it's impossible to have a well-functioning family with so many children, it's been my experience that large families, especially in the rural areas, can prove to be, for the most part, healthy families.

The children in these families learn to cooperate and share with each other. They also learn the importance of doing their share of the household tasks, as well as the importance of helping others.

When children vary in age from four to seventeen, it can create some challenges. Their parents have to be individualized in the way they treat their children, and take into account their developmental level when interacting with each child. This can create complications or conflict among the children. They often argue about what's fair and what's not fair, and they argue about who receives preferential treatment. For instance, a 7-year-old may ask why he has to go to bed at 8:30 p.m., while his 15-year-old brother gets to stay up until 9:30 p.m. His mother can explain that younger kids need more sleep, or she can give him some other reasons. But, she needs to keep track of what rules apply to everyone and what rules apply to only some of her kids.

I've worked with families that have only one child, and I've worked with families that have anywhere from eight to ten children. Once, I worked with a family that had eleven foster children. They had an additional caretaker to help supervise the children.

Although this was a highly functional family, problems arose from having such a large family. The children acted out more each time a new child was placed in the home. I saw this dynamic repeat itself over the two-year period I was their therapist.

All of the children competed for attention, both negatively and positively. This created a situation in which the parents had to take respite from at least some of the kids on a frequent basis, in order to prevent burnout. Luckily, they had relatives close by who were also seasoned foster parents. These two families took turns providing respite for each other's kids.

Large families may have difficulty supervising all the children at once. Some parents rely on creative strategies and build playrooms attached to the house, so they can monitor the children more closely. The playrooms are attached to the main house with sliding glass doors and big windows. This enables the parents to supervise the kids from the living room or the kitchen area. These families can take other measures as well to try to ensure their children's safety. Still, it remains a challenge for the parents to meet everyone's needs at the same time.

There are benefits to having smaller families. A child may receive more attention from the parents. He may not have to compete for attention as much, and he may be able to maintain his behavior without too much parental supervision.

However, there may be negative side effects to having smaller families. The child may feel isolated and bored, and he may look toward negative peers at school for companionship. He may also lack the opportunity to develop his skills in cooperating and negotiating with other children.

Rural vs. Urban Families

I've found some differences between rural and urban homes as well. Sometimes, children prefer rural areas even if they come from the urban ghetto. Usually these children complain that there's nothing to do when they first move into the small towns. However, they eventually learn to appreciate the closeness they feel with others in these smaller communities.

Although there is less privacy, these children tend to benefit from the attention they receive in these small towns. People call them by their name when they go to the only gas station in town. They feel more validated and important because people notice and acknowledge them.

Children in the urban areas, however, also benefit from living in a larger community. There are more resources available to them.

However, children in urban areas are often pressured into joining gangs or exposed to other negative peer influences. They may feel lost in the big schools and feel insignificant, unless they act out in some way.

Girls or Boys?

In biological families, you can't select the sex of your child. After all, you're not a kangaroo. If a mother kangaroo gives birth to a male baby, she can choose to have a girl kangaroo the next time around. But, humans don't have this option.

However, in foster and adoptive homes, you do have the option of choosing whether you want a girl, a boy or both. I think it is more exciting to have a mixture of girls and boys. Unfortunately, it may also be a challenge to mix them in foster homes or adoptive homes. This is especially the case when some of them have been sexually abused in the past.

This doesn't mean that girls don't try to sexually act out with other girls or that boys don't try with other boys. However, it's been my experience that children act out more often with others of the opposite sex. Even if none of the children were sexually abused in the past, they may still sexually act out with each other.

Suppose you have a 15-year-old girl and a 15-year-old boy in your foster home. They may be more prone to sexually act out with each other due to their developmental level. They may be curious about sex or they may be under peer pressure to experiment with each other sexually. They may decide to give into the pressure, due to each other's "accessibility."

Girls aren't better than boys or vise versa, but different foster parents may prefer working with one sex or the other. Some parents want to work with teenage girls only. However, these parents, foster mothers especially, want to work with girls because they understand girls better and can relate to them better.

Some foster parents want to work only with boys, even though boys tend to be more aggressive than girls. Some say they prefer boys because they don't have to worry about the boys getting pregnant (Of course, they have to worry about their boys getting the girls pregnant!). Some of them want to raise boys just because they never had any boys in their biological family.

Sibling Placements

Many child placing and child protective agencies ask the foster parents and the adoptive parents to take in children from the same sibling groups. Sometimes, parents agree to accept two siblings at the same time. However, they sometimes agree to take in three or four kids from the same family.

Based on my experience, children should be allowed to remain with their biological siblings when in their best interest. It's already difficult for them to lose their parents. To lose their siblings as well often proves to be more than they can bear emotionally.

Conversely, there are concerns over placing siblings together. There are problems that may be accentuated by their biological ties, and some problems that may be specific to just siblings. Siblings bring with them their history and their habits of relating to one another from their biological homes. It's often very difficult for foster parents or adoptive parents to teach them new ways of relating to each other.

Case Study

I worked with foster parents who had two boys from the same family. The older brother, Zach, was used to bullying and hitting the younger brother, Thomas, to get his way. Thomas, in turn, was used to crying and tattling on Zach. They replayed this dynamic over and over again in their new home.

Their foster parents and I decided to separate the two and have them share rooms with other children in the home. The two brothers were encouraged to play with each other under the foster parents' supervision. Also, they were not allowed to go into each other's rooms without their parents' permission for any reason.

In therapy, I talked to the boys about using assertive communication, rather than physical aggression, to get their way. I also encouraged Thomas to speak up for himself and to protect himself. Additionally, I reminded Thomas to turn to his foster parents if he felt he was in real danger.

After a while, when the boys would have minor arguments, their foster parents let them handle their conflicts on their own. When the boys got along, their parents praised them and acknowledged their appropriate interaction.

After about three months, Zach ceased to be physically aggressive toward his brother, as well as the other children in the home. Thomas learned to speak up for himself, and he stopped tattling on Zach considerably.

Introducing the New Child to Your Family

Unfortunately, many foster kids have to move several times between various foster homes and residential treatment centers before they settle down at one placement for an extended period of time. Each time they move they have to get used to the new parents, new siblings and new rules.

Therefore, it is important to introduce the new child to all the family members. I believe it's a good idea to have one of the kids already familiar with the house show the new child around. Sometimes, it's better for a kid to tell a new child about the household rules, etc.

You should supervise this process and allow the child giving the tour to do most of the talking with the new child. You can insert things or clarify the rules when needed.

Sometimes, parents have their new teenagers sign a contract, indicating that they understand and agree to the household rules. The rules are often displayed in a common area, so their teenagers can easily refer to the list, just in case they "forget" the rules.

Should Family Therapy be Mandatory?

Some child placing agencies mandate that therapists provide family therapy for their foster children and to include everyone in the family during the sessions. I believe this is a good idea, especially for children who are recently placed in a home.

However, there are some cases where forcing a child to attend family sessions is counter-therapeutic. For example, many teenagers close up during the family sessions, even if I can't stop them from talking during the individual sessions. Some teenagers do not bond with their foster parents, whether it's because they want to remain "loyal" to their biological families or because they just think their foster parents won't understand them.

I'm not recommending that we give up on family therapy altogether with these families. But, perhaps, postponing family sessions, until there's some understanding between all the participants, may be the best approach for everyone.

The Importance of Providing Closure

Because foster children often move from place to place, they may develop many issues from having to move repeatedly. They may have problems bonding with others and developing long-lasting intimate relationships.

Their placement may break down for various reasons, and sometimes due to their inappropriate behaviors. Whatever the reason, it's extremely important for them to have closure with their foster family, as well as their case manager, therapist, etc. before moving onto another placement.

I work with many children who suffer from not having the closure they need during these moves. In therapy, they repeatedly talk about their ex-foster home. They even talk about their ex-therapists. It takes time, effort and much coordination to make closure possible for these children. However, considering the emotional costs of lacking closure, it's a good investment for us to put in the time and effort for their welfare in the long run.

Choosing Your Family

Families from different socioeconomic and educational backgrounds have their strengths and weaknesses as well. One isn't necessarily better than the other. A family's strength depends on many things. There is no guarantee which combination works best for a given child.

However, as I've pointed out already, there are options when it comes to either fostering children or adopting them. You can choose your foster child's race, sex or age. You can choose to have a small or large foster family, and you can choose to live in an urban or rural area. These are just some of the things you may want to consider when deciding to become either a foster parent or an adoptive parent (or both, in some instances).

You can turn to your case manager at the child placing agency or the adoption agency for help during this process. The case manager can help you weigh the pros and cons between these different types of families so that you may choose what you think will best meet your needs and your children's needs.

There are some things that you just can't choose about your family. However, you can choose to have a healthy and safe family for your children.

Chapter 25

Conclusion

As I continue to work with children, I'm always amazed at their resiliency. Most of my clients have been traumatized in some way. Sometimes they have minor problems, such as school problems or friendship problems. Other times they have more serious problems such as sexual or physical abuse. But most of them prove to be more strong and resilient than most adults I know. Perhaps, it's because they're children and they're more receptive to change. They may not possess the defenses that adults often do. My young clients actually listen to me and follow my suggestions—at least sometimes!

You may indeed "mess up" in your efforts to relate to your children differently. But you can start over again and try harder the next time you have a chance to relate to them positively. Children are resilient and, sooner or later, they can change if you make the investment and if you persevere in your efforts to help them change for the better.

I wrote this book because of my desire to help children foremost. I wanted to help make this a better place for children where they can be healthy, happy and safe. But I need your help, because without your love, your hard work and your dedication to children, I'd be ineffective in my efforts. Together, we can create a better world, a better place for our children.

Appendix

‒►══◉═►‒

You may contact the following resource agencies for more information on various aspects of reporting, prevention and treatment of child abuse and neglect.

American Bar Association
National Legal Resource Center on Children and the Law
1800 M Street, N.W., Suite 200
Washington, DC 20036
(202) 331-2250

American Public Welfare Association
810 First Street, N.E., Suite 500
Washington, DC 20002
(202) 682-0100

Childhelp USA
6463 Independence Avenue
Woodland Hills, CA 91367
(800) 4-A-CHILD
(800) 422-4453

Child Welfare League of America
440 First Street, N.W., Suite 310
Washington, DC 20001
(202) 638-2952

National Association of Counsel for Children
1025 Oneida Street
Denver, CO 80220
(303) 321-3963

National Center for Missing and Exploited Children
1835 K Street, N.W., Suite 700
Washington, DC 20006
(800) 843-5678
(202) 634-9821

National Clearinghouse on Child Abuse and Family Violence
1155 Connecticut Avenue, N.W., Suite 400
Washington, D.C. 20036
(202) 505-3422

National Committee for Prevention of Child Abuse
332 South Michigan Avenue, Suite 950
Chicago, IL 60604
(312) 663-3520

National Organization for Victim Assistance
1757 Park Road, N.W.
Washington, D.C. 20010
(202) 232-6682

Parents Anonymous
6733 South Sepulveda Boulevard, Suite 270
Los Angeles, CA 90045
(213) 410-9732
(800) 421-0353 or (800) 352-0386 (for California only)

Parents United/Daughters and Sons United/
Adults Molested as Children United
P.O. Box 952
San Jose, CA 95108
(408) 280-5055

U.S. National Center on Child Abuse and Neglect
Department of Health and Human Services
P.O. Box 1182
Washington, DC 20013
(202) 245-0586

Victims of Child Abuse Laws (VOCAL)
P.O. Box 11335
Minneapolis, MN 55412
(800)-84VOCAL

Additional Resources

The following is a list of other organizations serving children and families.

Children's Defense Fund
25 E Street N.W.
Washington, D.C. 20001
(202) 628-8787

Families First
250 Baltic Street
Brooklyn, NY 11201
(718) 237-1862

National Adoption Information Clearinghouse (NAIC)
P.O. Box 1182
Washington, D.C. 20013-1182
(703) 352-3488
(888) 251-0075

National Foster Parent Association, Inc.
P.O. Box 81
Alpha, OH 45301-0081
(800) 557-5238

National Organization of Single Mothers
P.B. Box 68
Midland, NC 28107
(704) 888-2337

Travis County Family Violence Task Force
Project Courage
P.O. Box 1748
Austin, TX 78767
(512) 708-4423

Bibliography

⊷≡○⊜≡⊶

American Psychiatric Association, *Diagnostic and Statistical Manual of Mental Disorders-Fourth Edition*, American Psychiatric Association, Washington, DC, 1994.

Berry, J., *Every Kid's Guide to Making Friends*, Grolier Enterprises Inc., Danbury, CT, 1987.

Besharov, D.J., *Recognizing Child Abuse: A Guide for the Concerned*, The Free Press, NY, 1990, p. 16.

Clark, R.E. and Clark, J., *The Encyclopedia of Child Abuse*, Facts on File, NY, 1989, p. 134.

Fees, B.S., Stockdale, D.F., Crase, S.J., Riggins-Caspers, K., Yates, A.M., Lekies, K.S. and Gillis-Arnold, R., "Satisfaction with Foster Parenting: Assessment One Year after Training," *Children and Youth Services Review*, 20, 4, 1998, pp. 347-363.

Garcia, M.M., Shaw, D.S., Winslow, E.B. and Yaggi, K.E., "Destructive Sibling Conflict and the Development of Conduct Problems in Young Boys," *Developmental Psychology*, 36, 1, 2000, pp. 44-53.

Greenwalt, B.C., Sklare, G. and Portes, P., "The Therapeutic Treatment Provided in Cases Involving Physical Child Abuse: A Description of Current Practices," *Child Abuse and Neglect*, 22, 1, 1998, pp. 71-78.

Haesler, M., "The Absent Father: Gender Identity Considerations for Art Therapists Working with Adolescent Boys," *Art Therapy: Journal of the American Art Therapy Association*, 13, 1996, pp. 275-281.

Maxmen, J.S. and Ward, N.G., *Essential Psychopathology and Its Treatment*, W.W. Norton and Company, NY, 1995, p. 443.

Prendergast, W.E., *Sexual Abuse of Children and Adolescents: A Preventative Guide for Parents, Teachers, and Counselors*, Continuum, NY, 1996, pp. 106-138.

Shaffer, D., *Developmental Psychology*, Brooks/Cole Publishing, Pacific Grove, CA, 1993, pp. 64, 241-264.

Yancey, A., "Identity Formation and Social Maladaptation in Foster Adolescents," *Adolescence*, 27, 108, 1992, pp. 818- 831.

Index

A

Abuse
  behaviors caused by, 122–23, 191
  physical, 62, 121–26, 204
  and punishment, 63
  sexual, 47–48, 73, 83, 85–86, 91, 93, 122, 204
Acting-out
  and sexual activity, 73, 93, 103, 110–11, 199
Activities, extra-curricular
  advantages of, 75
ADHD. *See* Attention-Deficit/Hyperactivity Disorder
Affection
  showing, 73–75
Aggression
  in children, 90, 96–98, 101
  intervention in physical, 97–98
  physical, 121
  and punishment, 98
  towards animals, 90, 92–94, 101
Alcohol abuse, 104
Allegations
  documentation of, 116–17
  of sexual abuse, 73, 116–17
Animals
  aggression towards, 93–94, 101
Anxiety. *See also* Separation Anxiety
  causes of, 159, 169–70
  in children, 83, 98, 138
  and compulsive behaviors, 158, 163–65

coping with, 168–69
  and encopresis, 158
  and enuresis, 158
  and fear, 175
  and hoarding, 165
  and hyperactivity, 158
  and nightmares, 158
  and obsessive thoughts, 161–63
  problem-solving for, 167–68, 169
  and stealing, 165
  symptom of, 158–70
  as symptom of abuse, 104
Argumentativeness, 88–89
Attention-Deficit/Hyperactivity Disorder (ADHD)
  and behaviors exhibited, 86
  children with, 12, 85–87
  and distraction, 89
  and inattentiveness, 87–88
  and logical consequences, 89
  symptom of, 85–86
  treatment of, 86, 89

B

Bed-wetting. *See* Enuresis
Behaviors
  and Attention-Deficit/Hyperactivity Disorder, 85–86
  changing, 72
  compulsive, 158, 163–65, 169
  divorce, effects on, 132
  oppositional, 86
  parents' response to, 49, 58, 61, 89

positive, 70, 72
  problematic, 29–30, 54, 83–203, 93–94, 121, 129, 177
  rationalization of, 92
  regressive, 104, 142–46
  and self-esteem, 186–87
Berry, Joy
  Every Kid's Guide to Making Friends, 148–49
Big Brothers-Big Sisters, 193
Blame
  self, 26, 122–23
Blended families, 136
Bonding
  and family meetings, 79–80
  and family members, 136
  as parenting skill, 26–27
  and recreational activities, 79
  with stepchildren, 136
Boredom
  effects of, 77–78, 198
  and sibling conflict, 152–53, 155
Boundaries
  and limits, 55–58, 110, 121
  and rules, 55–58, 136
  and touching, 114-15
Boy Scouts, 77

C

Caregiver. *See* Parents
Caretakers. *See* Parents
CASA. *See* Court Appointed Special Advocate
Change
  parents creating, 25–26

Character building
in children, 46–47
definition of, 47
Child-centered, 27–29
Child placement agencies,
203
Child protective agencies,
108–09, 119
Children
aggression in, 90, 96–98,
101
and anxiety, 83, 98, 138,
158–70
argumentative, 88–89
with Attention-Deficit/
Hyperactivity Disorder
(ADHD), 12
and bed-wetting, 142–46
behavioral needs of, 11–12
behaviors of, 29–30, 54,
70, 83–203, 93–94,
121, 129, 177
blaming self of, 26, 122–
23
and choices, 57, 88–89
in communities, 191
and compassion, 47
and conduct problems,
90–102
and coping skills, 68–69
and depression, 83, 127–
30, 137, 177
development of, 197
and divorce, 83, 177
and empathy, 47–48
and encopresis, 142–46
and enuresis, 142–46
environment of, 46, 101,
135
in extra-curricular
activities, 75
fear in, 104, 106, 138
hope for, 118–19
individuality of, 46
in legal system, 191–92
and living skills, 65
and making friends, 148–
49
mental health of, 70, 83–84
motivating, 42–44, 57
physical abuse of, 121–26
and problem-solving, 66–
67
problems affecting, 11–12
resiliency of, 204

and responsibility, 42–44,
45–46, 52–53
rights of, 191
self-esteem of, 70–75,
182–88
and sensitivity, 47
and separation anxiety,
171–76
and sexual abuse, 47–48,
73, 83, 85–86, 91, 93,
103–20, 204
and social skills, 65–69
supervision of, 42
and time concept, 107,
119
witnessing abuse of
parent, 124–26
Choices
and children, 57, 88–89
and consequences, 57
Closure
providing, 140–41, 202
Cognitive development
concrete operations stage,
22
formal operations stage, 22
four stages of, 21–24
and morality, 94
preoperational stage, 22
sensorimotor stage, 22
stages of, 21–24
Communication
assertive, 69, 151
and divorced family
members, 135
and I-statements, 149–50
as parenting skill, 31–37
and social skills, 149
three areas of, 34–36
Community Service Clinic,
Arlington, TX, 13
Compassion, 47–48, 100
Compulsive behaviors, 158,
163–65, 169
Concrete operations stage, 22
Conduct problems
in children, 90–102
signs of, 90–91, 100–01
Confidentiality
and privacy, 189–90
Consequences
and consistency, 135–36
and following through, 102
legal, 92–93, 101
logical, 36, 49–54

natural, 49–54
and problem-solving, 68
and punishment, 68, 99
and rewards, 49
Consistency, 29–30, 135–36
Content mastery classes,
179, 181
Coping skills
in children, 68–69
Court Appointed Special
Advocate, 15, 192
Criminal activities. See
Illegal activities

D

Death
accidental, 137–40
children's response to,
137–38
and closure, 140–41
concept of, 137, 141
and depression, 128
in families, 137–38
and illness, 137–38, 141
Depression
in children, 83–84, 127–
30, 137
death causing, 128
divorce causing, 177
symptoms of, 127–28, 129
Developmental psychology,
21
*Diagnostic and Statistical
Manual of Mental
Disorders-Fourth
Edition* (DSM-IV),
83–84
Disclaimer, 17–18
Dishonesty. *See also* Lying,
99–100, 101, 116, 121
Disorders
symptoms of, 83–84
Distraction
and Attention-Deficit/
Hyperactivity Disorder
(ADHD), 89
as response to boredom,
77–78
Divorce
and behaviors, 132
cause of, 109–10, 119
and custody, 134, 135
and depression, 129, 177
effect on children, 83,
131–36, 192–93

and guilt, 132
reactions to, 142
and regressive behavior, 142
and separation anxiety, 172–74, 175–76
suggestions to parents, 132–33
therapy for coping with, 134–35
and visitation, 132, 135
DSM-IV. *See Diagnostic and Statistical Manual of Mental Disorders-Fourth Edition*
Dyslexia, 177–78, 181

E
Empathy, 47–48, 101, 102
Encopresis
and anxiety, 158
causes of, 121, 145
definition of, 142
and self-esteem, 144
symptoms of, 104
Enuresis
and anxiety, 158
causes of, 121, 145
definition of, 142
embarrassment of, 143–44
responses to, 145–46
and self-esteem, 144
symptoms of, 104, 142–46
Environment
of children, 46, 101, 135
Erikson, Erik, 168
Ethnicity
and multi-racial families, 194–97, 203
and tolerance, 195
Every Kid's Guide to Making Friends (Berry), 148–49
Extra-curricular activities. *See also* Recreational activities
and anxiety relief, 168–69, 170
benefits of, 96
children in, 75

F
Family
blended, 136
death in, 137–38
dynamics of, 17
foster, 26, 65, 116, 121, 192, 193, 201
large, 197–98, 203
meetings, 79–80, 191
multi-racial, 194–97
recreational activity of, 78–79
rural, 198–99, 203
small, 197–98, 203
therapy for, 17, 117–19, 126, 134, 137–38, 140–41, 146, 155, 169, 201–02
time together as, 78–79
types of, 136, 192–94, 197–200, 202–03
urban, 198–99, 203
Fears
and anxiety, 175
children's, 104, 138
of dark, 160
as result of abuse, 106
Feelings
expression of, 39–41
normalization of, 118
validation of, 41, 68–69, 107–08, 164, 169, 175, 176, 188
Formal operations stage, 22–23
Foster care
children in, 26, 65, 98, 116, 121, 192, 193, 199, 201–03
children introduced to, 201, 202–03
institution of, 65, 116
parents, 26, 98, 116, 121, 192, 193, 199
Friendship, 148–49, 151

G
Gang-affiliation, 90, 94–96, 101, 199
Gender, 199–200, 203
Girl Scouts, 77

H
Hoarding, 165–67, 169
Hope, 118–19
Hospice, 137, 141
Humor, 36, 72
Hyperactivity
and anxiety, 158
and Attention-Deficit/Hyperactivity Disorder (ADHD), 85–88, 128
and depression, 127, 128, 129
as symptom of abuse, 104

I
I-statements, 150–51
Illegal activities
legal consequences for, 92–93, 101
responsibility for, 91–92
illness
and anxiety, 175
terminal, 137, 141
Incest
divorce resulting from, 109–110
and sexual abuse, 105–06, 110, 119
therapy for victims of, 117–18
Individuality, 46
Insomnia, 104, 121, 127, 138, 1158
Isolation, 104, 121, 127, 148, 198

J
Jefferson, Thomas, 47

K
Kids. *See* Children

L
Law
and child advocacy, 191–92
and reporting of abuse, 108–09, 111, 118, 119
Legal consequences, 92–93, 101
Limits
and boundaries, 57–58
Lincoln, Abraham, 47
Listening
active, 151
and validation, 164
Logical consequences
and anxiety, 169
and conduct problems, 100–01
and parenting, 36, 49–54

and Attention-Deficit/
Hyperactivity Disorder
(ADHD), 89
follow-through of, 53, 136
and natural consequences,
53
and sibling conflict, 155
time-outs, 62
Love
expressions of, 75–76, 133
Lying. *See also* Dishonesty,
90

M
Mental health
of children, 70
diagnosis of, 83–84
Morals, 92, 94
Motivation
and encouraging children,
42–44, 46, 57
lack of, 179–80, 181
and punishment, 51
Multi-racial families, 194–97

N
Narcissism, 100, 102
National Center on Child
Abuse and Neglect, 62
Natural consequences
and conduct problems,
100–01
and logical consequences,
53
and parenting, 49–54
and teenagers, 54
Nightmares, 103, 121, 158,
160–61, 169–70

P
Parenting
basic skills, 25–26, 76–80
being child-centered, 27–
29
and bonding, 26–27
and character-building,
46–47
and communication, 31–37
and conduct problems,
100–01
and confidentiality, 189–
90
and consistency, 29–30
and coping skills teaching,
68–69

and distraction techniques,
76
and expressing feelings,
39–41
fundamental skills, 21–80
and humor, 36, 72
and praising, 34–39, 72
and punishment, 52, 60–
62
and self-esteem in
children, 182–84, 186–
87, 188
and sibling conflict, 154–
55
as single parent, 192–94
Parenting Center, Fort
Worth, TX, 13
Parents
adoptive, 26, 98, 121,
199–200, 203
and aggression in children,
98
biological, 26, 98, 135–36,
199–200
communication by, 31–37
consistency needed by, 29
divorced, 131–36
foster, 26, 98, 116, 121,
192, 193, 199–200
insecurity of, 34–35
non-custodial, 135–36
and promises, 150–51
and response to behavior,
49
as role models, 42, 69, 151
role of, 26
separated, 131–36
therapeutic methods, 12–13
Peer pressure, 149, 151, 198,
199
Perfectionism
aims toward, 122
and self-esteem, 184, 188
Physical abuse
of children, 121–26
definition of, 62
determining existence of,
121–22
help for, 124
and sexual abuse
differentiation, 122, 126
witnessing of, 124–26
Physical characteristics
and impact on self-esteem,
184–85, 188

Piaget, Jean, 21
Play therapy, 137, 153
Post-traumatic Stress
Disorder (PTSD), 123–
24, 126
Praise
appropriate use of, 37–39
as motivation, 46, 72
as parenting skill, 34–35
and self-esteem, 186–87
for siblings, 154–55
Pregnancy, 103
Preoperational stage, 22
Privacy
and confidentiality, 189–
90
and teenagers, 189–90
Privileges
and rewards, 58–60
Problem-solving
for anxiety, 167–68, 169
and children, 66–67
and consequences, 68
in divorce, 132
elements of, 67–68
Promises
keeping, 150–51
Psychology
developmental, 21
Erikson on, 168
impacts, 15, 119
reverse, 190–91
PTSD. *See* Post-traumatic
Stress Disorder
Punishments
and abuse, 63
and aggression, 98
and consequences, 99
corporal, 60–62, 64
and motivation, 51
and parenting, 52
and threats, 52
and time-outs, 51, 60–62

R
Rape Crisis, Fort Worth,
TX, 14
Recreational activities. *See
also* Extra-curricular
activities
and sibling conflict
resolution, 153–54, 155
in blended families, 136
and bonding, 79
as family activity, 78–79

Regressive behaviors
  causes of, 104
  and divorce, 142
  enuresis as, 142–46
Responsibility
  and choices, 54
  teaching children, 43–44,
    45–46, 52–53, 54, 90
Rewards
  and behaviors, 78
  and consequences, 49
  and consistency, 135–36
  and privileges, 58–60
Role models
  parents as, 42–46, 151
  siblings as, 128–29, 154,
    155
Role play, 149–50, 151
Roosevelt, Eleanor, 47
Rules
  and boundaries, 55–58,
    136
  and safety, 114–15, 118
  and touching, 115

S
Safety
  personal, 114–15
School
  and academic
    performance, 127
  advocacy in, 191
  and behavioral problems
    in, 90, 104, 177–81, 204
  content mastery classes
    in, 179, 181
  and homework, 89
  problems at, 177–81
  and social skills, 147
  and special education,
    178–79
Self-esteem
  and behaviors, 186–87
  in children, 70–75, 182–88
  and depression, 127
  encopresis, effects on, 144
  enuresis, effects on, 144–
    45
  increasing, 70–71
  influences on, 188
  low, 104, 182–88
  parenting children with
    low self-esteem, 182–84
  and peer pressure, 149,
    151, 198, 199

and perfectionism, 184
and physical
  characteristics, 184–85
and praising, 186–87
and social skills, 147–48
Sensitivity, 47–48
Sensorimotor stage, 22
Separation
  and guilt, 132
  of partners, 131–36, 132
  reactions to, 119, 142
Separation anxiety. See also
  Anxiety
  and divorce, 172–74,
    175–76
  effects of, 174–75
  reasons for, 174–75
  symptoms of, 171, 174–
    75
Sexual abuse
  and acting-out, 73, 91, 93,
    103, 110–11, 199
  allegations of, 73, 116–17
  and blaming self, 122–23
  of children, 47–48, 73,
    83, 85–86, 103–20, 204
  disclosure of, 106–07,
    108–09
  documentation of, 116–17
  and incest, 105–06, 110,
    119
  legal reporting of, 108–
    09, 111, 118, 119
  perpetrators of, 106–07,
    111–13, 122
  and physical abuse
    differentiation, 122, 126
  psychological effects of,
    119
  signs of, 103–04, 119
  and social isolation, 148
  therapy for victims of, 117
Sexually transmitted disease,
  103
Sibling conflict, 152–55
Sibling rivalry. See Sibling
  conflict
Siblings
  and conflict, 152–55
  and placement of, 200–
    201
Social functioning, 65
Social skills
  age-appropriate, 65-69,
    147–51

and communication, 149
and self-esteem, 147–48
sexual abuse impact on,
  148
Socialization, 46
Special education, 178–79
Stealing
  and anxiety, 165–67, 169
  causes of, 122
  as conduct problem, 90,
    101
Suicidal, 104, 127, 128,
  129, 148

T
Tattling, 156–57
Texas, 13, 14, 65
Therapeutic parenting
  definition of, 12–13
  special issue related to,
    189–203
Therapy, professional
  and families, 17, 117–19,
    126, 134, 137, 140–41,
    146, 155, 169, 201–02
  and individuals, 17, 118,
    119, 126, 133, 134,
    141, 146, 155, 169–70
  seeking out, 17, 83, 105,
    117, 130
Time
  concept of in children,
    107
Time-outs
  and logical consequences,
    62
  and punishments, 51, 60–
    62, 63–64
Touching
  implications of, 73
  rules of, 115
  types of, 73

U
University of Texas,
  Arlington, 13

V
Violence, 63, 64

Y
YMCA, 193
YWCA, 193

To inquire about scheduling K. H. Kim, LMSW-ACP for seminars or interviews, please contact the publisher at the address below. You may e-mail her with your comments regarding *Therapeutic Parenting* at khkim@hopewellpublishing.com. However, please note that due to the volume of requests, she is unable to respond to individual letters or phone calls.

Hopewell Publishing
12356 Donovan
Austin, Texas 78753, USA
www.hopewellpublishing.com

Therapeutic Parenting

ORDER FORM

*10% DISCOUNT on orders of $50 or more.
*30% DISCOUNT on orders of $500 or more.
*On cost of books for fully prepaid orders.

- **Fax orders**: (512) 836-1607
- **Telephone orders**: (512) 750-5098. Please have your credit card ready.
- **On-line orders**: www.hopewellpublishing.com
- **Postal orders**: Hopewell Publishing, 12356 Donovan, Austin, TX 78753, USA

Please send the following books:

Title	Quantity	Price	Total
_____	_____ @ $_____	= $_____
_____	_____ @ $_____	= $_____
_____	_____ @ $_____	= $_____

SUBTOTAL $_____

Less discount @ (____)% $_____

TOTAL COST OF BOOKS $_____

Texas residents add 8.25% sales tax $_____

Shipping and handling $_____

(Please pay in U.S. funds only.) **TOTAL ENCLOSED** $_____

Shipping Costs:
* Book Rate: $3.50 for the first book and $1 for each additional book (Please note that surface shipping may take up to 2 weeks.)
* To ship outside U.S. or to ship by airmail: $6.50 per book
* For bulk shipments call us at (512) 750-5098

Payment:
___Check, ___Money Order, ___Credit Card: ___VISA, ___MasterCard, ___Discover

Card Number: _____

Name on Card: _____ Expiration Date: ____/____

Name of Company: _____

Name: _____

Address: _____

City: _____ State: _____ Zip: _____

Telephone: (_____) _____